Tea & CAKE

Tea &
CAKE

perfect pairings for brews and bakes

LIZ FRANKLIN

Photography by **ISOBEL WIELD**

RYLAND PETERS & SMALL
LONDON • NEW YORK

Senior Designer Toni Kay
Editors Céline Hughes and Stephanie Milner
Production Controller Mai-Ling Collyer
Art Director Leslie Harrington
Editorial Director Julia Charles
Publisher Cindy Richards

Prop Stylist Polly Webb-Wilson
Food Stylist Lizzie Harris
Indexer Vanessa Bird

First published in 2014.
This revised edition published in 2020 by
Ryland Peters & Small
20–21 Jockey's Fields
London WC1R 4BW
and
341 E 116th St, New York NY 10029
www.rylandpeters.com

10 9 8 7 6 5 4 3 2 1

Text © Liz Franklin 2014, 2020
Design and photographs
© Ryland Peters & Small 2014, 2020

UK ISBN: 978-1-78879-217-2
US ISBN: 978-1-78879-208-0

Printed and bound in China

A CIP record for this book is available from
the British Library.

US Library of Congress Cataloging-in-
Publication Data has been applied for.

NOTES
• Both British (metric) and American
(imperial plus US cups) are included
in these recipes for your convenience;
however it is important to work with one
set of measurements and not alternate
between the two within a recipe.
• All spoon measurements are level unless
otherwise specified.
• All eggs are medium (UK) or large (US),
unless otherwise specified. Uncooked
or partially cooked eggs should not be
served to the very old, frail, young children,
pregnant women or those with compromised
immune systems.
• When a recipe calls for the grated zest of
citrus fruit, buy unwaxed fruit and wash well
before using. If you can only find treated fruit,
scrub well in warm soapy water before using.
• Ovens should be preheated to the specified
temperatures. We recommend using an
oven thermometer. If using a fan-assisted
oven, adjust temperatures according to
the manufacturer's instructions.

CONTENTS

Introduction **6** All About Tea **8** Breakfast Teas **20**
Calming Teas **38** Refreshingly Different Teas **58**
Afternoon Teas **78** Dinner Party Teas **108**
Index **126** Credits **128**

INTRODUCTION

I grew up in North Yorkshire, where tea was tea. At my house, it was made with loose leaves in a teapot and 'mashed' (brewed) until it was dark and robustly flavoured. It was served with a smidgen of milk, nothing else. It was wet and warm and sometimes so strong you could almost stand a spoon up in it, the sort of tea that builders are notoriously supposed to thrive on, but that was how it was then – back in the days when pasta meant spaghetti hoops in a tin and olive oil came from the chemist!

As I began to discover the myriad teas available, I came to appreciate that different teas have unique characteristics and flavours, and can be suited to a wide array of occasions.

A cup of tea can help perk us up when we're flagging a little, calm us down when we're restless, lift us when we're feeling low, help us celebrate with friends and soothe us when we feel under the weather. Quality teas can bring out the best in the food we choose to eat alongside our chosen cuppa, just as the right fine wine can enhance a plate of food.

Learning to appreciate that a first flush is nothing to do with a visit to the bathroom, that orange pekoe doesn't actually taste of orange, and that plucking isn't only for the eyebrows, has been one of the most enjoyable experiences I have had over the years. Matching the multitude of stunning teas that are now available to us with lovely homemade sweet treats has been an absolute delight. I hope you will enjoy the recipes and revel in new discoveries just as much as I have.

After water, tea is the most widely consumed drink in the world, yet it is often thought of as being a characteristically British drink. It is true that tea has been sipped and slurped all over Britain for several centuries, but to trace the real origins of tea, we have to travel back around 5,000 years to China.

Legend would have it that while travelling one day Emperor Shen Nung was sitting beneath a tree waiting for his servant to boil some drinking water. A light breeze stirred, and a number of leaves from the tree blew into the water. The Emperor is credited with being the father of Chinese medicine and an expert in pharmacology, so the newly created infusion naturally aroused his curiosity and he drank it. The tree in question was *Camellia sinensis* – the evergreen plant whose leaves we now cultivate to produce tea – and the brew was the first cup of tea.

Although we have no real proof of this story, tea containers and related paraphernalia were found in ancient tombs dating back to 206 BC and the Han dynasty, although it was several hundred years later, during the the Tang dynasty, that tea found its place as the national drink of China.

By the 8th century, touring Japanese Buddhist monks had introduced tea to Japan from China and the Chinese were trading tea with Tibet along the famous 5,000 km Ancient Tea Horse Road. Business soon spread further into Asia and beyond.

Fast forward a few hundred years to the late 16th century, and tea had reached European shores. Portuguese traders and missionaries to the Far East are thought to have brought tea back to their own countries, but it was the Dutch who first began shipping tea to Holland, where it became a fashionable drink. From there, tea drinking spread to other western European countries, although high production and transportation costs meant that tea remained a drink available only to the wealthy population.

In 1662 in England, the marriage of Catherine of Braganza (a Portuguese princess and tea enthusiast) to King Charles II made tea fashionable in the Royal Court, and from there it continued to gather a following among aristocracy. As tea began to reach less affluent sections of the population, much mystery, mayhem and very likely the odd murder or two ensued. The costliness of tea was partly down to huge government-imposed taxes, so criminal gangs resorted to smuggling and often adulteration of the leaves in order to keep up with demand for supplies for the working classes.

Ironically, although we now know that tea is a healthy drink, it was suspected at the time that tea drinking could lead to infirmity and depression and was discouraged among those who had to earn their living. However, it soon became accepted that tea was a more suitable drink than alcohol when it came to wetting the whistle of the working classes.

Eventually, the government lowered the taxes and they were finally lifted in 1861. And so began the rise and rise of tea drinking in Britain.

ALL ABOUT TEA

We are increasingly discovering the health benefits and enjoyment to be had from drinking tea. However, the differences between types of teas can be quite confusing at first, so I have outlined the main types of tea here. Some of the recipes include teas that aren't technically teas at all, in the strictest sense of the word, in that they are not made from the leaves of *Camellia sinensis*; they are the caffeine-free infusions of various herbs and spices, often referred to as 'tisanes'.

TYPES OF TEA

There are six main types of tea, but within these types there are a whole host of varieties. Once you get to grips with the characteristics and flavours of the different types, you will find that an exciting new adventure has begun.

Black Tea

Usually strong and earthy, black teas are fully oxidized and are produced using one of two methods. In the orthodox method, the fresh tea leaves are withered for several hours and then rolled, which releases oils that coat the surface of the still-green leaves. The leaves are left until fully oxidized and then fired to prevent them from rotting. The alternative method is a mechanical process known as CTC (crush, tear, curl) and experts believe that on the whole, teas produced using this method are of a lower grade.

Black tea is used as the base of many popular flavoured teas. Earl Grey is a blend of black tea infused with oil from the bergamot orange. English and Irish breakfast teas are based on the leaves of full-bodied black teas and India's favourite Masala

Chai is a sweet and aromatic blend of black tea, milk and spices that is gaining in popularity around the world now. Lapsang Souchong, Assam, Darjeeling, Ceylon and Keemun are all well known varieties of black tea.

Green Tea

Unlike black teas, green teas do not go through any form of oxidization (the chemical changes that happen after exposure to air). They can be first or second flush; using very tender buds and shoots from an early season crop or more robust from later crops. Initially they are allowed to wither in a dark place, which reduces the water content. In China, the leaves are usually then roasted and left to dry out. This process kills the enzymes in the leaves, which prevents any oxidization. In Japan, this is more commonly achieved by steaming the leaves before they are rolled and dried.

80 per cent of the world's green tea comes from China, and as such the leaves have really interesting names. Two of my favourite green teas are Pi Lo Chun (which translates as 'jade snail spring') and Chun Mee (which translates as 'precious eyebrows'), both so named because of the shape of their leaves. The famous gunpowder tea traditionally used in Moroccan mint tea is also a green tea.

Japanese green teas such as gyokuro and sencha are gaining in popularity around the world, and matcha green tea powder, the tea traditionally used in Japanese tea ceremonies, is now widely used to flavour ice creams, noodles and cakes. Research has uncovered amazing health benefits related to drinking green tea. Green teas are considered to have anti-aging and anti-bacterial properties. Drinking green tea on a regular basis can help to reduce levels of bad cholesterol in the body. As a natural source of antioxidants green tea is thought to help fight cancer, and investigations have also revealed that frequent consumption of green tea can aid weight loss.

A huge variety of flavoured green teas are now available to buy. I prefer to add my own natural flavourings to the tea – although I do love Jasmine tea, which is produced from an infusion of Jasmine flowers and green tea.

Oolong Tea

Oolong teas are partially oxidized, and therefore more processed than green tea but less so than black tea. They are essentially a hybrid of green and black tea, said to have been discovered by accident when a Chinese gardener was distracted by a deer that he subsequently killed and prepared to eat, forgetting about the tea that he had been brewing prior to his sudden diversion. Returning to the tea the next day, he found the leaves had changed colour due to partial oxidation – but he carried on and finished the tea anyway. The tea's increased aroma and depth of flavour made it a favourite – and so, oolong was born.

Oolong tea falls into two different categories. For darker oolongs, the leaves are tossed in bamboo drums to start the oxidization process. When they are 60–70 per cent oxidized, the leaves are dried. The lighter, greener oolongs are only 30 per cent oxidized and are wrapped in cloths and machine-rolled before being dried. Both have unique characteristics, and many tea aficionados believe oolongs to be the most distinctive and agreeable of all teas.

They are ideal for multiple steepings and it is said that the flavour of the tea gets better and better each time the pot is filled up. Dedicated oolong fans believe that the fourth or fifth steeping releases the best flavour – although you'd need a pretty strong bladder to get to your fifth cup without retiring.

Formosa oolong comes from Taiwan. Imperial formosa oolong is an especially acclaimed tea. Traditionally drunk by Taiwanese Buddhist monks, it is considered one of the best teas in the world.

Pu-erh Tea

Pu-erh teas are oxidized to a similar level as green teas, but are dark in colour and unique in that they go through a process known as post-fermentation. Traditionally, pu-erh comes from the Yunnan province in China and is gaining in popularity because one of its purported health benefits is that it is believed to aid weight loss. For 'raw' pu-erh, the processed tea is compressed into cakes and left to age for up to 50 years, making it very expensive. However, 'cooked' pu-erh is increasingly produced, which takes much less time to manufacture and involves the introduction of a special bacterial culture that speeds up the maturation.

Specialist tea suppliers will sell pu-erh tea cakes and bricks. The tea must be gently prised from the cake or brick, or the leaves will be damaged and this could have a negative effect on the flavour of the tea. The best tool to use for this delicate operation is a pu-erh knife, which is a special 'tea needle' that can be lightly inserted into the brick or cake and used to work the tea loose. However, loose leaf pu-erh is widely available from tea specialists, supermarkets, department stores and even health food shops.

White Tea

White tea is the least processed of all the teas and is generally the most esteemed. Only the topmost bud and leaves are picked from the bush, sometimes only the bud, and they are always first flush. The buds must be picked before they unfurl, are handled as little as possible and processed minimally. They are withered in the sunshine or, in bad weather, in a warm room. White teas are silvery in colour, have a mild flavour, are low in caffeine and have the highest antioxidant content of any of the teas.

Baihao yinzhen ('silver needle') and Pai Mutan, or Bai Mudan ('white peony') are particularly good white teas to look out for. Slightly sweet and deliciously mellow, silver needle is my own personal favourite tea.

Yellow Tea

Yellow tea is produced in a similar way to green tea, but the leaves are left to turn yellow before they are dried. Yellow tea is generally milder and sweeter than green tea.

It is one of the rarest types of tea and is relatively undiscovered in the west. Yellow tea has a sweet, mellow flavour and is particular to the Sichuan and Hunan provinces of China. It may take a little effort to get hold of some, but as you begin to discover and enjoy the world of specialist teas, you will realize it's one worth tracking down!

TEA EQUIPMENT

Strictly speaking, the only essential things needed to make tea are a receptacle of some sort (a cup, mug or heatproof glass), some form of tea and boiled water (good-quality tea leaves tend to sink, so you shouldn't be struggling with too many stray leaves). Of course, if you're using a teabag, you'll need something to fish the tea bag out once your tea is brewed to the desired strength. But when you discover the world of truly amazing teas that are available, making the tea itself becomes a really enjoyable part of the whole process. Pouring the

tea from a beautiful pot is a delight, and filling up a favourite tea stick or tea ball or making your own-blend tea bag is a real pleasure, so there are various pieces of equipment you might like to invest in. Tea paraphernalia often also makes a great gift. Here are a few ideas you might like to consider.

TEAPOT

Once upon a time, a teapot was as much a piece of essential kitchen kit as the saucepan or pot. When the tea bag came along, things changed. If you think of the importance and ceremonies associated with tea around the world, it seems a shame that tea-making in the west was ever reduced to simply sticking a tea bag willy-nilly into a mug, pouring boiling water over it and squashing it with a spoon. Thankfully, proper tea is making a well deserved return to the table! Teapots come in all shapes and sizes and a variety of materials, from the very beautiful to the practical. I think they become a little like a favourite mug or cup and tea will definitely taste different depending on what pot it is made in. It would be a shame to serve a delicate white tea from the sort of traditional Brown Betty teapot that is customarily associated with a strong breakfast brew, but there is something about those sturdy teapots that make them perfect for on the table alongside a cooked breakfast and lots of hot buttery toast and marmalade.

I like to serve delicate white teas and green teas in pretty china pots that reflect their delicate flavour, although I love glass for the flowering tea balls. Glass teapots now have better insulation, so they keep the tea hot, and it's interesting to watch tea leaves or a tea ball unfurl as the brewing process takes place.

My everyday teapot is a sturdier earthenware pot that's a sort of white version of the Brown Betty. Of course, in an ideal world you would have a teapot to match the type of tea you are making. There are some beautiful Asian-style teapots with handles that somehow make drinking Japanese teas a very special experience, but not all of us have the budget or the cupboard space!

A good all-purpose pot would be made from not-too-delicate china. Some people favour the teapots that come with built-in infusers, so that the tea doesn't over-brew, but if you're worried about that, you can scoop the tea into an infuser and clip it to the side of the pot, then remove it when you're happy with the strength of the tea. Whatever the preference, there's a teapot out there for everyone.

TEA BALLS, TEA STICKS AND INFUSERS

Tea balls, tea sticks and infusers make it easy to brew loose-leaf tea while keeping the leaves contained, making them as convenient as tea bags while still allowing you to enjoy your favourite loose-leaf tea. However, some tea experts argue that they restrict the movement of the leaves and therefore don't allow the true characteristics of the tea to come out in the brewing process. They can be used in a teapot or individual mug or cup, and come in all shapes and sizes, from the plain and practical to the ornate. They are usually made from stainless steel, although they do come in silver, for those for whom cost isn't a consideration!

TEA COSIES

Just as the teapot was once a household item, so too was the tea cosy. Whether knitted, crocheted, sewn or shop bought, from the plain and practical to the entertaining and elaborate, the purpose of the tea cosy was to keep the pot warm. Sceptics argue that a tea cosy won't make much difference to keeping a pot hot, and, of course, tea left to sit could become over-brewed and bitter as the tannins continue to be released, but there is something fun and cheery about a tea cosy, so it's down to personal choice as to whether you have one (or several) in your personal *batterie de thé*!

TEA CADDIES

Tea caddies, or canisters, have been around for as long as tea itself, and range from the everyday to the highly decorative, but essentially they do the necessary job of keeping the tea fresh, and therefore preserving its flavour. Premium teas can be bought in nice caddies, but are also increasingly sold in foil packages and ideally should be transferred to an airtight container upon opening.

STRAINERS, SQUEEZERS AND SUNDRIES

Pouring tea through a strainer into a cup does away with the risk of getting leaves in the cup and the embarrassment of trying to pick tea leaves out of your teeth. Good-quality tea leaves do sink to the bottom of the pot however, and so controlled pouring will help if you don't have a strainer to hand. They are inexpensive and easy to buy so a strainer is a good investment. Tea bag squeezers are a little bit of an indulgence, but they are a little more sophisticated than squashing the bag against the side of your cup with a spoon. There are also tea bag tidies, measuring and caddie spoons and all kinds of bits and bobs you can add to your kit as your enjoyment of fine teas unfolds.

HELPFUL TEA TERMINOLOGY

The science surrounding the harvesting, production, brewing and serving tea necessarily lends itself to a few pieces of jargon that you may come across when exploring the world of tea. As with wine and food, tea is often described by the accents of flavour found in the taste but there are also some technical terms that feature. Here are a few to get you started.

FANNINGS OR DUST

'Fannings' or 'dust' are mainly low-quality leftover leaves that are often used in tea bags.

FLOWERY

'Flowery' indicates that the tea includes buds and leaves, and is also a sign of good quality.

FLUSH

The term 'flush' is used to describe the tree's growing season, when it is pushing out new leaves. So a 'first flush' tea is produced using the very first tender buds and shoots, and is considered the most delicate in taste, although second flush tea leaves are thought to have a little more body. Subsequent flushes are used but generally not acknowledged.

ORANGE

Orange pekoe teas come under the orthodox black tea category and have a recognized grading system. Leaves are classified into larger leaf grades and 'broken' leaf grades, which are the smaller pieces. Legend has it that the term 'orange' came about when the East India Trading Company presented the tea to the Dutch royal family, the House of Orange, and subsequently went on to promote the tea as 'orange pekoe' to imply a royal warrant.

PICKING

'Picking', also known as 'plucking', happens between spring and autumn/fall, which is the growing season in countries such as China and northern India. In countries where the weather is more consistent, picking takes place all year round. The quality of the tea is determined by the number of leaves and buds that are plucked from each plant.

Tea can be graded by its country of origin – such as Darjeeling, Assam, China, Ceylon (Sri Lanka), and so on – but the grading of the leaves is also an important aspect of the tea-making process, as small leaves will brew at different rates to larger leaves and produce often very different results.

STEEPING

The essential process of soaking your tea leaves and ingredients in water. How you brew your tea comes down to personal preference but some teas, such as oolong are better suited to multiple steepings than others, and often result in an enhanced, richer flavour.

TIPPY

'Tippy' is an indication that the tea includes the highest proportion of buds, or 'tips', and is therefore of the highest quality.

BRINGING TEA TO THE TABLE

TEA PRODUCING REGIONS

From its origins in China all those centuries ago, major tea cultivation has now spread to the verdant hills, high mountains and coastal regions of a handful of countries. India, Japan, Sri Lanka and Taiwan join China as producers of the world's acclaimed teas.

China

The humid tropical and subtropical provinces of southern China holds the largest concentration of the country's tea estates. China produces so much tea that the well-known phrase 'not for all the tea in China' came about - meaning 'not at any price', although India has now become the world's biggest producer of tea.

India

Assam and Darjeeling are often thought of types of tea, when in fact they are the regions in which those teas are cultivated. Darjeeling tea carries a PGi certificate, which means that only teas cultivated, produced and processed within a specified area of Darjeeling can actually carry the name. Genuine Darjeeling tea should carry the official logo, introduced by the Tea Board of India. Darjeeling teas were primarily black teas, but now green, oolong and white teas are increasingly being produced.

Japan

Tea was originally introduced to Japan from China by Buddhist monks. Nowadays, Japan is renowned for its excellent green teas and the Shizuoka and Kagoshima regions are the principal producers.

Sri Lanka

Formerly known as Ceylon, Sri Lanka's humidity, temperatures and rainfall all help to produce high quality teas. Sri Lankan teas are largely black, and the Sri Lankan Board of Tea issue a quality mark to pure Ceylon teas.

Taiwan

Taiwan is an island situated off the south eastern coast of mainland China, originally known as

Formosa. Because the bushes are cultivated at comparatively low altitudes, the island produced a high percentage of oolongs.

BREWING THE PERFECT CUPPA

Tea aficionados all around the world argue about how to brew the perfect cuppa, but loose tea is generally considered to produce a better quality tea than bags. Loose teas are most often produced from the whole leaf and allow the user more control over the strength of the tea; more leaves in the pot will usually make a stronger tea. Loose-leaf tea can usually be steeped several times; some teas are even thought to benefit from it. Real tea connoisseurs will pour an initial amount of hot water into a teapot containing the leaves, then pour the water out, rather than simply

warming the pot before adding the leaves. The benefit of doing so is that any dust that is clinging to the leaves will be washed away, and the leaves are supposedly primed to swell, encouraging maximum flavour.

The Royal Society of Chemistry has published a guide to making the perfect cup of tea. They advise using freshly drawn water every time. When water boils, it loses some of its oxygen, and oxygen helps bring out the flavour of the tea. They recommend a ceramic teapot, as metal can sometimes taint the flavour of the tea.

The advice is to brew the tea for 3–4 minutes (although this would depend on the type of tea), since polyphenolic compounds (tannins) are released after this time which give the tea its colour and some of its flavour. However, leaving the tea to infuse for longer than this apparently introduces high molecular-weight tannins, which give the tea a bad aftertaste. I think this describes the bitter, over-brewed tea that we used to call 'stewed' in Yorkshire.

A MATTER OF MILK

Although many of the teas in this book are better without milk, the subject of when to add milk to teas that can take milk is a hotly contested one. Does the milk come first? Or the tea? Well, The Royal Society of Chemistry advocates that the milk (always fresh and chilled, and never long-lasting UHT) goes into the cup first, because degradation of the milk occurs if milk encounters temperatures above 75°C (167°F). The report says that 'if milk is poured into hot tea, individual drops separate from the bulk of the milk and come into contact with the high temperatures of the tea for enough time for significant denaturation to occur. This is much less likely to happen if hot water is added to the milk. Once full mixing has occurred, the temperature should be below 75°C (167°F).

Apparently, the perfect temperature at which to drink tea is 60–65°C (140–149°F) 'to avoid vulgar slurping which results from drinking tea at too high a temperature.'

The author of the report also goes on to say that 'to gain optimum ambience for enjoyment of tea, aim to achieve a seated drinking position, where quietness and calm will elevate the moment to a special dimension. For best results, carry a heavy bag of shopping – or walk the dog – in cold, driving rain for at least half an hour beforehand. This will make the tea taste out of this world.'

I hope that after reading this book and trying some of the teas, you will realize that tea can taste truly wonderful without having to haul heavy bags or schlep around the stormy streets beforehand!

BREAKFAST TEAS

*Work-day breakfasts may well mean grabbing
a quick bowl of cornflakes and speed-swishing a
teabag around in a mug before slurping it down and
heading out of the door, but when it comes to high
days and holidays, it makes such a lovely change to
slow down and take time to make something special
to share with family or friends. Start the day with
homemade chia seed muffins, fresh from the pan
crumpets, or even a slice of gorgeous just-baked
tart. And instead of that ever-so-slightly humdrum
cuppa, why not try one of a world of delicious
teas. And to think the day has only just begun!*

Orange pekoe tea with fat rascals

Despite the name, orange pekoe doesn't actually contain any orange. Orange pekoe is a term largely used to describe a category of black teas noted for their high quality, which mostly come from India and Sri Lanka. I first ate fat rascals in Harrogate, North Yorkshire, at Betty's Café Tea Rooms, but at the time they wouldn't divulge the recipe, so I bought one and did a bit of an autopsy on it at home. Here's what I came up with.

150 g/1 cup plus 2 tablespoons plain/all-purpose flour
150 g/1 cup plus 2 tablespoons self-raising/rising flour
1 teaspoon baking powder
130 g/9 tablespoons butter, cubed
90 g/scant ½ cup caster/superfine sugar
grated zest of 1 orange
grated zest of 1 lemon
1 teaspoon ground cinnamon
½ teaspoon freshly grated nutmeg
150 g/1 generous cup mixed dried fruit (I use currants, raisins and sultanas)
1 egg, beaten
50 ml/3 tablespoons milk
1 egg yolk
a pinch of salt
glacé cherries and blanched almonds, to decorate

MAKES 6

Preheat the oven to 200°C (400°F) Gas 6.

Sift both flours and the baking powder into a large bowl. Add the butter and rub into the flour until the mixture resembles fine breadcrumbs.

Add the sugar, orange and lemon zests, spices and dried fruit and mix well. Add the beaten egg and enough milk to bring the mixture together to a soft dough. Shape the mixture into 6 saucer-sized rounds, about 2 cm (5 in.) deep.

Mix the egg yolk, 1 tablespoon water and salt together to make a glaze and brush this over the fat rascals. Decorate with the cherries and almonds. Transfer to a non-stick baking sheet and bake for 15–20 minutes, or until golden brown.

Fat rascals are best served warm, either alone or with plenty of butter. They're also gorgeous served with vanilla-scented mascarpone.

FOR 1 POT OF TEA

3–4 teaspoons orange pekoe tea
sugar or honey, to taste
milk, to taste

Warm the pot and add the tea leaves. Pour in boiling water and leave to brew for about 4 minutes. Sweeten with sugar or honey and add milk, if desired.

Moroccan mint tea with apple, cinnamon and cardamom bourekas

Traditionally, Moroccan mint tea is brewed in a very specific way: the leaves are washed and the water is poured into the pot from a certain height, as is the tea, once brewed. This process adds oxygen, which is believed to draw out more flavour. Bourekas are crisp, golden little pastry parcels. Here I've used apple, cinnamon and cardamom: perfect for breakfast with the mint tea.

400 g/14 oz. crisp dessert apples
60 g/5 tablespoons butter
5 cardamom pods
50 g/¼ cup caster/
    superfine sugar
a pinch of salt
1 teaspoon ground cinnamon
grated zest and juice of
    1 small lemon
8 sheets of filo/phyllo pastry
    squares, about
    20 x 20 cm/8 x 8 in.
1 teaspoon caster/
    superfine sugar
2 tablespoons chia seeds

MAKES 8

Preheat the oven to 190°C (375°F) Gas 5.

Peel and core the apples and cut them into smallish dice. Melt half the butter in a large frying pan or wok and add the diced apples. Remove the seeds from the cardamom pods. Stir in the sugar, salt, cardamom seeds and cinnamon. Cook for about 5 minutes, or until the apples have turned golden and the juices have started to thicken. Add the lemon zest and juice and cook for 3–4 minutes, until the apples are soft. Remove from the heat and allow to cool.

In the meantime, take a sheet of filo/phyllo pastry and fold it in half, so that you have a rectangle two layers thick. Melt the remaining butter in a small saucepan. Brush the pastry lightly with butter. Place a tablespoon of the cooked, cooled apple in the bottom left-hand corner of the pastry. Lift the corner beneath it and pull it over the filling to form a triangle. Fold the pastry immediately to the left, so that it retains the triangle shape. Repeat the process, folding up and down, until the pastry is used up and you are left with a neat triangle. Place it on a non-stick baking sheet and brush lightly with butter. Repeat to make 7 more bourekas. Sprinkle each one with sugar and chia seeds and bake in the oven for about 8–10 minutes, until crisp and golden.

FOR 1 POT OF TEA

2 teaspoons green tea
a handful of fresh mint

Warm a teapot. Add the tea and mint and fill with boiling water. Allow to brew for about 3 minutes. Remove the mint and pour into cups.

Assam leaf tea with goji berry, chia seed and citrus muffins

Assam tea is one of the oldest varieties in the world; the bushes originally grew wild on the immense flood plains of the Brahmaputra River in the Assam region of India. Today, the steamy, hot conditions of the region still produce rich, full-bodied tea with distinctive small leaves and a malty flavour that makes it popular at breakfast time. Chewy red goji berries and crunchy chia seeds are full of antioxidants and other good stuff, and the bonus is that they taste really great. I love them sprinkled over a bowl of fruit and yoghurt for weekday breakfasts, but for a weekend treat, I make these lovely muffins and serve them with a seasonal fruit compote. On less virtuous days I just eat them warm from the oven with a generous slathering of butter. And a pot of good tea is never far away!

160 g/1¼ cups plain/
  all-purpose flour
2 teaspoons baking powder
50 g/¼ cup caster/
  superfine sugar
30 g/¼ cup chia seeds
50 g/⅓ cup dried goji berries
1 egg
100 ml/6½ tablespoons milk
1 teaspoon pure vanilla extract
100 g/6½ tablespoons butter,
  melted and cooled slightly
50 g/3 tablespoons fine-cut
  orange marmalade

a 6-cup muffin pan,
  or 6 freestanding muffin
  papers, lightly greased

MAKES 6

Preheat the oven to 180°C (350°F) Gas 4.

Put the flour, baking powder and sugar in a large bowl and mix well. Add the chia seeds and goji berries and stir them in.

In a separate bowl, beat the egg, milk and vanilla extract together. Add the slightly cooled butter and beat again. Gently but carefully mix the egg mixture into the dry ingredients, until fully incorporated. Spoon the mixture into the prepared moulds.

Bake for about 20 minutes, until the muffins are risen and golden and spring back when pressed lightly.

In the meantime, warm the marmalade a little in a small saucepan. Remove the muffins from the oven and leave to cool slightly before brushing the tops with a light glaze of marmalade.

Serve warm with a pot of Assam tea.

FOR 1 POT OF TEA

3-4 teaspoons Assam
  tea leaves
sugar or honey, to taste

Warm the pot and add the tea leaves. Pour in the boiling water, stir and leave to brew for 3–4 minutes. Sweeten with sugar or honey and serve with the warm muffins.

Prince of Wales tea with apple and cinnamon scones

Prince of Wales tea is a blend of black China tea originally created for Edward, Prince of Wales (the future King Edward VIII). In 1921, he granted Twinings permission to sell his personal blend using his royal title and they have done so ever since. It's quite a mild tea with a strong aroma, and it makes a perfect cuppa. These lovely apple scones make a very regal combination with the tea.

500 g/4 cups self-raising/rising
   flour, plus extra for dusting
100 g/6½ tablespoons butter,
   diced
a pinch of salt
50 g/¼ cup caster/
   superfine sugar
½ teaspoon ground cinnamon
1 Bramley apple, peeled,
   cored and diced
scant 300 ml/1¼ cups whole milk
1 egg and 1 tablespoon milk,
   beaten together

a 4-cm/1½-in. cookie cutter

MAKES 6–8

Preheat the oven to 200°C (400°F) Gas 6.

Sieve the flour into a large bowl and add the butter. Rub it lightly into the flour with your fingertips, lifting the mixture to aerate it as you work. When the mixture resembles fine breadcrumbs, add the salt, sugar and cinnamon and mix to combine. Stir in the apple.

Add just enough milk to bring the mixture together to form a soft (but not sticky) dough. Take care not to handle the dough too much or the scones will become heavy.

Lightly dust a clean work surface with flour and roll the dough out to about 3 cm (1 in.) thick. Stamp out rounds with the cookie cutter. Try to avoid re-rolling the dough, as this will make the scones heavy. Place the scones on a non-stick baking sheet and bake for about 12–15 minutes, until risen and golden. Leave to cool a little on a wire rack. They are lovely served warm.

FOR 1 POT OF TEA

3 Prince of Wales tea bags
sugar or honey, to taste
milk, to taste

Warm the pot. Add the tea bags and pour boiling water over. Leave to brew for 2–5 minutes. Sweeten and add milk as desired.

Passion Fruit and orange tea with sticky oat breakfast bars

If you like fruity notes in your tea now and again there are some really nice blends on the market. I'm not a big fan of the shop-bought fruity infusions that don't include tea as a base, but Lipton make a very nice green tea that is delicately flavoured with passion fruit, jasmine and orange, and other companies make a similar blend. These sticky oat bars are easy to make and packed with oats and seeds, so they make a great accompaniment to a cuppa for those of us who aren't big on breakfast, or are a little short on time in the mornings.

225 g/scant 1 cup butter
225 g/1 cup plus 2 tablespoons
  brown sugar
3 tablespoons honey
a pinch of salt
325 g/3¼ cups jumbo oats
2 tablespoons mixed seeds
  (such as sunflower, sesame,
  hemp, pumpkin or linseeds)
50 g/1 cup cornflakes

a 20 x 30-cm/8 x 12-in. baking
  pan, greased and lined with
  baking parchment

MAKES 15

Preheat the oven to 180°C (350°F) Gas 4.

Melt the butter, sugar, honey and salt together in a saucepan over gentle heat. Stir in the oats, seeds and cornflakes.

Spoon the mixture into the prepared pan and bake for 20–25 minutes, until golden and firm.

Leave to cool in the pan, then cut into squares.

FOR 1 POT OF TEA

1 passion fruit and orange
  tea bag per person
sugar or honey, to taste

Put a tea bag in each mug and pour over boiling water. Leave to brew for 2–5 minutes. Sweeten with sugar or honey, as desired.

Tea with crumpets

We all have our favourite brand of everyday, comfort tea – generally black tea, often made from lower-grade leaves and fannings, or dustings – and sometimes it's just what we fancy. Tea with a gutsy flavour and makes a good cuppa to start the day, especially alongside warm, freshly made crumpets with lashings of good butter.

350 ml/1½ cups milk
250 g/2 cups plain/
   all-purpose flour
a pinch of salt
2 teaspoons caster/
   granulated sugar
7 g/2 teaspoons dried fast-action/
   active yeast
½ teaspoon baking powder
1 tablespoon melted butter,
   plus extra for frying

metal crumpet rings

MAKES 8

Heat the milk in a saucepan until it is lukewarm. Mix the flour, salt and sugar together in a large bowl. Add the yeast and baking powder. Stir the butter and milk together, then pour it into the flour. Stir well and leave to rise for about 1 hour.

Grease the base of a frying pan/skillet with butter, set it over a medium heat and pop the crumpet rings into it. Spoon a little batter into each one and cook for a couple of minutes, until the mixture starts to set, little bubbles appear at the top and the bases are golden. Carefully remove the rings and turn the crumpets over. Cook for a further 2–3 minutes, until firm and golden. Wrap them in a clean dish cloth to keep them warm, and make the others in the same way. Serve warm with lots of butter and jam/jelly. To reheat, simply pop them in a toaster or cook under a hot grill/broiler.

FOR 1 POT OF TEA

2–3 tea bags
milk and sugar, to taste

Warm the teapot and add the tea bags. Pour over boiling water and leave to brew for 3–4 minutes. Add milk and sugar to taste.

Royal English breakfast tea with traditional fruit tea bread

English breakfast tea is usually a blend of black teas such as Assam, Ceylon and Kenya, although some tea companies prefer to use only Assam. Breakfast tea is usually quite strong and gutsy with malty, nutty overtones. It's one of the few teas I believe actually benefits from the addition of milk. Of course, English breakfast tea makes a great accompaniment to the classic English breakfast, but it's also really good with this lovely fruit tea bread, which I love to serve toasted and slathered with lots of butter.

350 g/3 cups mixed dried fruit

300 ml/1¼ cups freshly brewed Earl Grey tea, hot

400 g/3¼ cups self-raising/ rising flour

1 teaspoon baking powder

1 egg, beaten

a 900-g/2-lb. loaf pan, lightly greased and lined with baking parchment

MAKES 10–12 SLICES

Put the fruit in a large bowl and pour over the hot tea. Cover and leave to stand for several hours, preferably overnight.

When you are ready to bake the loaf, preheat the oven to 180°C (350°F) Gas 4. Sieve the flour and baking powder together into a large bowl. Add the soaked fruit and stir well. Beat in the egg until everything is thoroughly combined.

Pour the mixture into the prepared loaf pan and bake for about 1½ hours, or until a skewer inserted into the centre of the loaf comes out clean.

Leave to cool for 15 minutes or so, and then turn out onto a wire rack to cool completely.

FOR 1 POT OF TEA

3–4 teaspoons English Breakfast tea or tea bags

milk and sugar, to taste

Warm the pot. Add the tea bags and pour over boiling water. Leave to brew for 2–5 minutes. Sweeten to taste with sugar or honey and add milk as desired.

Mango-infused tippy green tea with fresh apricot tart

One of the leading factors in determining the flavour and caffeine content of a tea is the proportion of tips or leaf buds it contains. Tippy teas generally have a smoother, milder flavour and a higher caffeine content than teas with larger, mature leaves. Here, I've added dried mango to tippy green tea to give a subtle hint of fruitiness – an ideal match for a fresh apricot tart.

FOR THE PASTRY
175 g/1½ sticks soft butter
50 g/¼ cup caster/
    superfine sugar
a pinch of salt
1 egg yolk
250 g/2 cups plain/
    all-purpose flour

FOR THE FILLING
120 g/1 stick soft butter
a pinch of salt
120 g/⅔ cup caster/
    superfine sugar
2 eggs
120 g/1 cup ground almonds/
    almond meal
750 g/1 lb. 10 oz. fresh, ripe
    (but firm) apricots, quartered
    and stoned/pitted
5 tablespoons smooth apricot
    jam/jelly

*a 23-cm/9-in. tart pan with
    removable base, and
    baking beans*

SERVES 6–8

Preheat the oven to 180°C (350°F) Gas 4.

For the pastry, beat the butter, sugar and salt together until smooth. Add the egg yolk and stir until thoroughly mixed. Fold in the flour and bring it all together to form a smooth dough. Wrap in clingfilm/plastic wrap and set aside in a cool place while preparing the filling.

For the filling, beat the butter, salt and sugar together until light and fluffy. Stir in the eggs and beat until fully combined. Add the almonds and stir until they are fully incorporated and the mixture is smooth.

Roll out the pastry and use it to line the tart pan. Trim of the excess. Line the pan with the pastry and trim off the excess. Line with baking paper, fill with baking beans and bake the pastry blind for about 10 minutes, or until light golden and firm. Allow to cool.

Spread the filling in an even layer over the tart base. Arrange the apricots over the filling, facing up in concentric circles and close together. Bake the tart for about 45 minutes, until the filling is firm and golden. Remove from the oven and allow to cool. Finally, warm the apricot/jam jelly with 1 tablespoon water and brush it all over the apricots for a shiny glaze.

FOR 1 POT OF TEA

4 teaspoons tippy green tea
2 tablespoons thinly sliced
    dried mango

Warm a teapot. Add the tea and mango and fill with boiling water. Allow to brew for 4–5 minutes. Pour into tea glasses and add an extra slice of mango if desired.

CALMING TEAS

These days, it's so easy to get caught up in the hustle and bustle of everyday life. So often the day disappears and we haven't realised just how much pressure we've put upon ourselves. It's so nice every now and then, just to put the brakes on and relax. Of course sometimes we need a little help to wind down – and here are some great teas and tisanes which help do just that. Of course if you happen to have an irresistible banana and nutmeg custard brownie, or a crisp cardamom shortbread as an accompaniment... well then, you'll be laid back and in heaven all at the same time!

Chamomile flower tea
with vanilla butter cookies

Chamomile flowers are renowned for their calming and digestive properties. There are many brands of chamomile infusions, and you can create your own with dried chamomile flowers. These little buttery, vanilla-speckled cookies go well with any kind of chamomile tea.

2 vanilla pods
200 g/1¾ sticks soft butter
100 g/½ cup caster/superfine
  sugar, plus extra for dusting
300 g/2¼ cups plain/
  all-purpose flour

*2–3 cookie sheets, lined
  with baking parchment*

MAKES 20–25

Preheat the oven to 180°C (350°F) Gas 4.

Split the vanilla pods lengthwise and scrape out the seeds. Cream the butter, vanilla seeds and sugar until smooth, then stir in the flour until fully combined.

Break off pieces of dough about the size of a walnut and roll each one into a ball. Place on the prepared cookie sheets, leaving a little gap between each to allow for slight spreading. Push the tines of a fork into the dough to flatten it slightly and bake for about 10–13 minutes, until golden and firm. Dust with caster/superfine sugar.

Transfer to a wire rack to cool. Store in an airtight container until ready to serve.

FOR 1 POT OF TEA

2 teaspoons dried
  chamomile flowers
honey or sugar, to taste

Warm a teapot and add the chamomile. Fill with boiling water and infuse for 5 minutes. Sweeten as desired.

Rooibos and vanilla tea with banana and nutmeg custard brownies

The slightly sweet and nutty flavour of rooibos is complemented by vanilla; I think the two make a perfect combination. Pair a cup or two with these deliciously different brownies and the stresses of the world just fade away...You can buy rooibos teabags already infused with vanilla, but it's easy to make using fresh tea and a vanilla pod too, whichever you prefer.

20 g/4 teaspoons butter
450 g/2¼ cups caster/
    superfine sugar
50 g/1½ oz. dark chocolate
100 g/¾ cup cocoa powder
4 eggs, beaten
100 g/¾ cup plain/
    all-purpose flour
1 teaspoon baking powder
2 very ripe bananas, mashed

FOR THE CUSTARD LAYER
250 g/1 cup mascarpone
4 egg yolks
100 g/½ cup caster/
    superfine sugar
freshly grated nutmeg

a 20 x 30-cm/8 x 12-in.
    rectangular roasting pan
    or cake pan, lightly greased

MAKES 15

Preheat the oven to 180°C (350°F) Gas 4.

Melt the butter, sugar, chocolate and cocoa powder together in a large heatproof bowl set over a pan of barely simmering water, or heat gently in a microwave. Remove from the heat and leave to cool slightly.

Stir in the eggs. Add the flour and baking powder and stir again until smooth. Add the mashed banana and mix well. Pour the mixture into the prepared pan.

For the custard layer, beat the mascarpone, egg yolks and sugar together until smooth. Drizzle the mixture randomly across the chocolate layer. Scatter the custard mixture with grated nutmeg. Bake for about 35 minutes, until firm but still slightly fudgy.

Leave to cool in the pan, then cut into squares.

FOR 1 POT OF TEA

3 teaspoons rooibos tea
    (or use tea bags)
1 plump vanilla pod
sugar or honey, to taste

Warm the teapot and add the tea. Fill it with boiling water. Split the vanilla pod lengthwise and scrape out the seeds. Add them to the pot along with the pod. Give everything a gentle stir and leave to infuse for 3–4 minutes. Sweeten to taste and pour into cups.

Lemon balm tea with clotted cream and raspberry brulée tartlets

Lemon balm has a lovely, delicate lemon flavour and is known for its calming properties. If you have some in the garden, making this delightful, gently aromatic tea will be easy: just infuse some green or white tea with a few of the leaves. I've paired it with these delicious little tarts; it's a combination I love to serve on sunny summer afternoons.

FOR THE SHORTCRUST
150 g/1 cup plus 2 tablespoons plain/all-purpose flour, plus extra for dusting
150 g/1 stick plus 2 tablespoons butter
75 g/⅓ cup caster/superfine sugar
75 g/½ cup plus 1 tablespoon rice flour
grated zest of ½ lemon

FOR THE FILLING
1 vanilla pod
2 egg yolks
200 g/scant 1 cup clotted cream
80 g/⅓ cup caster/superfine sugar
a pinch of flaky sea salt
250 g/2 cups fresh raspberries
3 tablespoons icing/confectioners' sugar

6 tartlet pans with removable base, about 6.5 cm/2½ in. diameter

a cooks' blow torch

MAKES 6

Preheat the oven to 180°C (350°F) Gas 4.

Rub together the flour, butter, sugar and rice flour until the mixture looks like breadcrumbs. Stir in the lemon zest and bring it together to form a dough. Chill until firm, then roll out on a lightly floured surface and line the pans, then return them to the fridge to chill.

Split the vanilla pods lengthwise and scrape out the seeds. Beat the egg yolks, clotted cream, sugar, vanilla seeds and salt until smooth.

Bake the shortcrust bases for 6–8 minutes, until firm and pale golden. If the shortcrust has risen up slightly, simply push it back carefully against the edges with a teaspoon. Remove from the oven and scatter the raspberries over the bases. Pour in the custard filling. Bake for 8–10 minutes for the fairy cake size, or 10–15 minutes for the larger size. Remove from the oven and leave to cool.

Sprinkle a fine layer of icing/confectioners' sugar over the top of each tart and caramelize carefully with a blow torch, taking care not to burn any raspberries that may be peeping out of the custard. Serve within a couple of hours, so that the brûlée top remains crisp.

FOR 1 POT OF TEA

3–4 teaspoons green or white tea, or tea bags
small handful lemon balm leaves
honey or sugar, to taste

Warm the pot and add the tea. Add the lemon balm leaves and pour over boiled, slightly cooled water. Infuse for 5 minutes. Sweeten as desired.

African honeybush tea with orange and rosemary cake

Honeybush is a cousin of rooibos, and therefore not technically a true tea. Just like rooibos, it is cultivated in South Africa's Eastern Cape and Western Cape provinces. Honeybush has a similar flavour, but is slightly sweeter, and is also caffeine free. Its name derives from the blossoms of the bush, which smell of honey. Sweetening the tea with honey adds a further depth of flavour, and eating a slice of this lovely orange and rosemary cake with it makes it even better!

320 g/2½ cups plain/
 all-purpose flour
2 teaspoons baking powder
150 g/¾ cup caster/
 superfine sugar
3 eggs
200 ml/¾ cup whole milk
120 g/1 stick butter,
 melted and cooled
grated zest of 2 oranges
 and juice of 1
1 tablespoon finely chopped
 fresh rosemary
4 tablespoons marmalade

*a 20-cm/8-in. cake pan with
 removable base, greased and
 lined with baking parchment*

SERVES 8–10

Preheat the oven to 180°C (350°F) Gas 4.

Sieve the flour and baking powder into a large bowl. Stir in the sugar.

In a separate bowl, whisk the eggs and milk together with the cooled melted butter. Stir lightly but thoroughly into the flour mixture. Stir in the orange zest and juice, taking care not to overmix. Fold in the chopped rosemary needles. Spoon the mixture into the prepared cake pan and bake for 50–55 minutes, until the cake has risen and is golden brown, and a skewer inserted into the centre comes out clean.

Leave to cool in the pan for 20 minutes or so, then turn out onto a wire rack and leave to cool completely.

Push the marmalade through a fine sieve/strainer and heat it gently in a small saucepan or pot. Brush the mixture evenly over the cake.

Store in an airtight container.

FOR 1 POT OF TEA

3–4 teaspoons African
 honeybush tea
honey, to taste

Warm the pot and add the tea. Pour over boiling water and leave to brew for 5–6 minutes. Sweeten with honey.

Olive leaf tea with pine nut and rosemary cookies

Olive leaf tea is an unusual, soothing sort of brew. It is said to have all kinds of amazing health benefits; the jury is still out on this one, but given the amazing health properties that olives contain, it seems reasonable to think that Mother Nature might have squeezed a few good things into the leaves as well. These crunchy pine nut cookies with just a hint of rosemary are delicious and so easy to make.

100 g/¾ cup pine nuts
120 g/1 stick soft butter
100 g/½ cup caster/
    superfine sugar
a pinch of salt
1 teaspoon very finely chopped
    fresh rosemary
150 g/1 cup plus 2 tablespoons
    plain/all-purpose flour

MAKES 15

Preheat the oven to 180°C (350°F) Gas 4.

Put the pine nuts in a large pan over medium heat and cook for 2–3 minutes, until toasted and golden, stirring regularly to prevent them burning. Remove and leave to cool.

Beat the butter, sugar and salt together until light and fluffy. Add the chopped rosemary and flour and stir until it is fully incorporated and the mixture is smooth. Add the pine nuts and stir to combine.

Place tablespoons of the mixture on a non-stick cookie sheet, spaced out well to allow room for the cookies to spread. Bake for about 8–10 minutes, until golden and firm. Remove from the heat and transfer to a wire rack to cool. The cookies will crisp up as they cool. Store in an airtight container until ready to serve.

FOR 1 POT OF TEA

1 heaped teaspoon
    olive leaf tea leaves
    (a little goes a long way)
sugar or honey, to taste

Warm the teapot and add the tea. Pour over boiling water and brew for 5 minutes. Serve with sugar or honey to sweeten.

Manuka honey tea with honey and banana bread

Manuka honey is a wonderful product with lots of health-giving properties, and makes a lovely sweetener for tea. Simply make a pot of green tea and sweeten with honey to taste, but let the water cool slightly first, as boiling water is said to destroy some of the benefits. For days when you want a quick cuppa, Clipper makes manuka honey tea bags, which are very nice. This cake is lovely served just as it is, but a layer of cold, creamy butter definitely lifts it to another level.

120 g/1 stick butter
100 g/½ cup caster/
    superfine sugar
4 tablespoons runny honey
2 eggs, beaten
250 g/2 cups self-raising/
    rising flour
2 very ripe bananas, mashed

*a 900-g/2-lb. loaf pan,
    greased and lined with
    baking parchment*

SERVES 6

Preheat the oven to 180°C (350°F) Gas 4.

Put the butter and sugar in a large bowl and beat until smooth and light. Add the honey and beat well. Add the eggs, a little a time – you can add a little flour too, if the mixture curdles. Stir in the remaining flour, and then the mashed bananas.

Spoon the mixture into the prepared pan and bake for about 1 hour 15 minutes, until it has risen and is golden and a skewer inserted into the centre comes out clean.

Leave the cake to cool in the pan for 20 minutes or so, then turn out onto a wire rack and leave to cool completely.

○ ···

FOR 1 POT OF TEA

3–4 teaspoons green tea
    leaves (or use 3 manuka
    honey tea bags)
manuka honey, to taste

Warm the pot and add the tea. Pour over boiling water and leave to brew for 3–4 minutes. Sweeten to taste with manuka honey.

Kaffir lime leaf tea with caramelized pear and thyme cake

Kaffir lime leaves add a lovely flavour to tea; I often use them to add flavour to a pot of white tea. Fresh leaves are best for this recipe, and you should be able find them quite easily in Asian food stores. At a pinch you could use dried, which are often found in the Asian section of major supermarkets, but the flavour isn't quite as fresh and pronounced. This pear cake is sticky and lovely, and the fragrant tea makes a perfect match.

280 g/2 sticks plus
   3 tablespoons butter
280 g/1½ cups caster/superfine
   sugar, plus extra for dusting
4 firm but ripe pears, peeled,
   cored and diced
4 eggs, beaten
280 g/2¼ cups self-raising/
   rising flour
1 tablespoon fresh thyme leaves

a 20 x 30-cm/9 x 5-in. deep
   roasting pan or cake pan,
   lightly greased

MAKES 10

Preheat the oven to 180°C (350°F) Gas 4.

Place 30 g (1¼ oz.) of the butter and 30 g (1¼ oz.) of the sugar in a non-stick frying pan/skillet over medium heat and cook until the sugar has dissolved. Add the diced pear and cook for about 5–8 minutes, until the pear is golden and caramelized. Leave to cool a little.

Beat the remaining butter and sugar together until light and fluffy. Add the eggs a little a time, adding a little flour too if the mixture curdles, until the mixture is smooth and all the eggs have been incorporated. Stir in the remaining flour. Add the pears and their buttery juices, along with the thyme.

Spoon the mixture into the prepared pan and bake for about 40 minutes, until the cake has risen and is golden and springy.

Leave it to cool in the pan. Dust with sugar and cut into squares to serve.

o···

FOR 1 POT OF TEA

3 teaspoons white tea
4–5 fresh kaffir lime leaves,
   lightly crushed
sugar or honey, to taste

Warm the teapot and the white tea and lime leaves. Fill the teapot with boiling water. Give everything a gentle stir and leave to infuse for 4–5 minutes. Sweeten to taste and pour into cups.

White sweet tea (Pai mu tan) with cardamom shortbread

Pai mu tan is a seriously delicious tea. Also known as White Peony, it comes from a variety of tea known as Narcissus or Chaicha, grown in the Fuijian province of China. A white tea, it is made from the unopened tea buds and the two earliest leaves to sprout, which are then left to wither and dry in the sun. It has a lovely naturally sweet, floral flavour and is one of my absolute favourites. Pai mu tan is a great tea to drink alone or alongside all manner of treats, but these delicately flavoured shortbreads somehow go so well – they make two graceful goodies together, I think.

120 g/1 stick soft butter
160 g/1¼ cups plain/
   all-purpose flour
60 g/⅓ cup caster/superfine
   sugar, plus extra for dusting
a pinch of salt
seeds from 5–6 cardamom pods,
   crushed

MAKES 20–24

Preheat the oven to 160°C (325°F) Gas 2.

Put all the ingredients in a large bowl and work until the mixture comes together to form a smooth dough. Shape it into a long sausage shape with a diameter of about 3 cm (1¼ in.), and wrap in clingfilm/plastic wrap. Refrigerate for about 30 minutes, until firm.

Cut the sausage into discs about 5 mm (¼ in.) thick and place on to non-stick cookie sheets, leaving space between each one for the shortbreads to spread.

Bake for about 15 minutes, until firm and golden. Cool on a wire rack, dust with sugar and store in an airtight container.

FOR 1 POT OF TEA

6 teaspoons Pai mu tan
   tea leaves
sugar or honey, to taste

Warm the teapot and add the leaves. Pour over water that has been boiled and slightly cooled. Leave to brew for 4–5 minutes. Sweeten to taste if necessary.

Fennel tea with lemon and almond financiers

Financiers are delightful little cakes that are very similar to friands, but financiers are generally made with beurre noisette (butter that is heated to a lovely amber colour and an appealing nutty aroma). The name 'financier' is thought to come from the fact that they resemble bars of gold, or perhaps because they were popular in the cafés in the financial district of Paris. I love fennel tea, although it's not technically a tea, but an infusion. You can buy fennel tea bags or buy empty bags to create your own tea; simply whizz some fennel seeds up in a blender and add a tablespoon to each bag.

70 g/½ cup ground almonds/
    almond meal
30 g/¼ cup plain/
    all-purpose flour
a pinch of salt
120 g/1 generous cup
    icing/confectioners' sugar
grated zest of 2 lemons
100 g/6½ tablespoons butter
3 egg whites
50 g/½ cup flaked/
    slivered almonds

*6 mini loaf pans or small muffin
    moulds, lightly greased*

MAKES 6

Preheat the oven to 180°C (350°F) Gas 4.

Mix the ground almonds/almond meal, flour, salt and sugar together in a large bowl. Stir in the lemon zest.

Melt the butter in a small saucepan and leave it over the heat until it turns to an amber colour and gives off a nutty aroma. Remove it from the heat and leave to cool slightly. Whisk the egg whites until frothy and light (you don't need to whip them to stiff peaks as you would if you were making meringues).

Trickle the butter into the dry ingredients and add half the egg whites. Mix lightly, and then add the remaining egg whites and continue to mix until fully incorporated.

Spoon the mixture into the prepared pans and scatter the flaked/slivered almonds over the top. Bake for about 15 minutes, until they are risen and golden and spring back when pressed lightly.

Serve warm, or leave to cool completely.

○··

FOR 1 POT OF TEA

2 fennel tea bags
sugar or honey, to taste

Warm the pot and add the tea bags. Pour over boiling water and leave to infuse for about 5 minutes. Sweeten with sugar or honey and serve.

REFRESHINGLY DIFFERENT TEAS

I absolutely love the teas in this section – they really do show how deliciously different teas can be and how simple herbs and spices can make wonderful brews too. Sweet basil tea is such a delicate infusion, but one that is as surprising as it is sensational; the result of a very happy accident. Add treats such as white chocolate and redcurrant brownies, raspberry and clotted cream whirls, and Caribbean rum cake and you really will be on Cloud Nine.

Jasmine flowering tea
with little custard tarts

Flowering tea never ceases to bring a smile to my face. The little flower bundles are made from dried tea leaves, which are wrapped and then tightly bound around one or more dried flower blossoms. When the boiling water is added, the bundle slowly unfurls to reveal the flower at the centre. It's no gimmick either – they make lovely tea! Every bundle can be used up to three times without the tea becoming bitter or too weak, so if you're having friends for afternoon tea, all you need is a glass teapot and you can watch the pretty spectacle unfold. Creamy, nutmeg-topped custard tarts encased in crisp, wafer-thin pastry are an elegant accompaniment to this very distinctive tea, and make afternoon cake-and-cuppa time very special indeed.

FOR THE PASTRY
175 g/1½ sticks soft butter
50 g/¼ cup caster/
    superfine sugar
1 egg yolk
250 g/2 cups plain/all-purpose
    flour, plus extra for dusting

FOR THE FILLING
2 egg yolks
2 whole eggs
250 ml/1 cup double/
    heavy cream
1 vanilla pod
50 g/¼ cup caster/
    superfine sugar
freshly grated nutmeg

*six 5-cm/2-in. tartlet pans
    with removable base*

MAKES 6

For the pastry, cream the butter and sugar together until light and fluffy. Stir in the egg yolk until fully combined. Lightly fold in the flour until a soft, smooth dough forms. Roll out on a lightly floured surface to a thickness of about 2 mm (⅛ in.) and cut out six rounds about 6 cm (2½ in.) in diameter. Line the tartlet pans, taking care to press the mixture into the corners. Refrigerate for 30 minutes.

Preheat the oven to 160°C (325°F) Gas 2. Beat the egg yolks, whole eggs and cream together until smooth. Split the vanilla pod lengthwise and scrape out the seeds. Stir the sugar and vanilla seeds into the eggs. Remove the tartlet cases from the fridge and place them on a baking sheet. Fill the cases with the custard mixture and grate a little fresh nutmeg over the top of each one. Bake for about 20 minutes, until the filling is set and golden. Leave to cool, then turn out of the pans and serve.

FOR 1 POT OF TEA

1 jasmine flowering tea bundle

Warm a glass teapot or heatproof glass jug/pitcher. Add the tea bundle and pour in very slightly cooled boiled water. In 2–3 minutes, the bundle will have unfurled and the tea will be ready to drink. Refill the pot up to three times.

White tea pearls with raspberry and clotted cream whirls

White tea pearls are lovely, and make an exquisite cup of tea. The leaves are carefully rolled into pearls and left to dry in the sun. When steeped, they unravel, releasing their lovely, fresh flavour and all those precious antioxidants. A special tea deserves a special accompaniment, and these buttery crisp whirls filled with clotted cream and raspberries fit the bill wonderfully.

250 g/2 sticks soft butter
200 g/1⅔ cups plain/
    all-purpose flour
50 g/½ cup cornflour/cornstarch
50 g/scant ½ cup icing/
    confectioners' sugar
1 teaspoon pure vanilla extract

FOR THE FILLING
300 g/1¼ cups clotted cream
250 g/2 cups raspberries
caster/granulated sugar,
    for dusting

2 baking sheets, lined
    with baking parchment
a piping/pastry bag
    with a star nozzle/tip

MAKES ABOUT 10

Preheat the oven to 180°C (350°F) Gas 4.

Mix the butter, flours, icing/confectioners' sugar and pure vanilla extract together until it forms a smooth dough. Spoon the mixture into a piping/pastry bag and pipe oval shapes about the size of a large egg onto the prepared baking sheets. Bake for about 15 minutes, until golden. Remove from the oven and leave to cool for a few minutes, then transfer to a wire rack until completely cold.

To serve, sandwich together with clotted cream and raspberries and dust lightly with sugar.

FOR 1 POT OF TEA

3 teaspoons white tea pearls
sugar or honey, to taste

Warm the teapot and add the white tea pearls. Pour over boiled water that has cooled slightly. Brew for 4–5 minutes. Sweeten with sugar or honey. This is a lovely, delicate tea, so adding milk isn't really a good idea.

Sweet basil tea with white chocolate and redcurrant brownies

Basil is associated with all things Italian, and usually savoury. But I had a notion one day that the leaves might make an interesting infusion, and my instinct paid off, because I fell in love with this lovely tisane. These white chocolate and redcurrant brownies seem to be a big hit with everyone who tries them. The white chocolate gives them a delicious flavour, and the almonds add a lovely soft, dense texture without them being heavy. I think this is a combination you'll be delighted you tried.

250 g/2 sticks butter
400 g/2 cups caster/
    superfine sugar
200 g/7 oz. white chocolate
4 eggs, beaten
200 g/1⅔ cups ground almonds/
    almond meal
100 g/¾ cup plain/
    all-purpose flour
1 teaspoon baking powder
100 g/⅔ cup redcurrants
icing/confectioners' sugar,
    for dusting

a 23-cm/9-in. square cake
    pan, greased and lined
    with baking parchment

MAKES 36

Preheat the oven to 180°C (350°F) Gas 4.

Put the butter, sugar and white chocolate in a microwave-proof bowl and microwave at medium-high for 1 minute. Stir and return the mixture to the microwave for a further 30 seconds, until fully melted. Leave to cool slightly, then stir in the beaten eggs.

Add the almonds, flour, baking powder and redcurrants, and mix well. Pour the mixture into the prepared pan. Bake for about 30 minutes, until firm and golden. Leave to cool, then cut into bite-size squares. Dust with icing/confectioners' sugar and serve.

FOR 1 POT OF TEA

3–4 handfuls fresh basil
    leaves
2 teaspoons sugar, or to taste

Put the basil leaves and sugar in the pot and pour in the water. Stir gently and leave to infuse for 3–4 minutes. Pour into cups and add more sugar to taste, as desired. It needs a little sugar to bring out the delicate flavours; start with a very small amount and adjust accordingly.

Cinnamon-scented black tea with Caribbean rum cake

The main difference between black tea and other types is the greater oxidation of the leaves; this means that black teas hold their flavour for much longer, and are often mixed with strong spices and flavourings. Here, I've used a robust black tea and infused it with a cinnamon stick. This glorious rum-soaked cake will accompany your slightly spiced cuppa perfectly.

250 g/2 sticks soft butter
250 g/1¼ cups caster/
   superfine sugar
4 eggs, beaten
250 g/2¼ cups ground almonds/
   almond meal
100 g/¾ cup plain/
   all-purpose flour
2 teaspoons baking powder
90 ml/6 tablespoons good-quality
   dark Caribbean rum

FOR THE SYRUP
100 g/½ cup caster/
   granulated sugar
50 ml/3 tablespoons good-quality
   dark Caribbean rum

a 24-cm/9½-in. ring-shaped
*   cake pan, greased*

MAKES 10–12 SLICES

Preheat the oven to 180°C (350°F) Gas 4.

Beat the butter and sugar together until light and fluffy. Add the eggs a little at a time until fully incorporated. Stir in the almonds, flour and baking powder and mix until smooth. Beat in the rum.

Spoon the mixture into the prepared pan and bake for about 1 hour, until it is risen and is golden and springs back when pressed lightly in the centre. Leave to cool in the pan for about 10–15 minutes.

In the meantime, put 100 ml (⅓ cup) water, the sugar and rum in a saucepan and heat until the sugar is melted. Bubble for 1–2 minutes until the mixture is slightly syrupy, then remove from the heat.

Turn the cake out of the pan and place on a wire rack set over a plate. Make pin pricks in the surface of the cake and spoon the syrup over until fully soaked into the cake. Any syrup that runs through will be caught on the plate and can be re-applied. Leave to cool completely before serving.

o···

FOR 1 POT OF TEA

black tea leaves
   (I love Yunnan)
cinnamon sticks
sugar or honey, to taste

Take a scoop of black tea in a tea ball and place in a tall mug with a cinnamon stick. Pour over boiled water and leave to infuse. Sweeten with the tiniest amount of sugar or honey, which helps balance the cinnamon flavour.

Ginger tea with sticky molasses and pumpkin cake

This is definitely one for gingerholics. If you need to sweeten the tea, I think honey is a better choice in this instance, as it will add another dimension to the duo.

320 g/2½ cups plain/
　all-purpose flour
1 teaspoon bicarbonate
　of soda/baking soda
1½ teaspoons ground ginger
200 g/1 cup dark molasses/
　turbinado sugar
100 ml/scant ⅓ cup golden syrup
100 g/6½ tablespoons butter,
　melted
3 eggs, beaten
150 g/⅔ cup cooked pumpkin,
　puréed (or use canned)
120 g/4 oz. stem/candied ginger,
　roughly chopped
butter, to serve

*a 900-g/2-lb. loaf pan, lightly
　greased and lined with
　baking parchment*

MAKES 10–12 SLICES

Preheat the oven to 180°C (350°F) Gas 4.

Put the flour, bicarbonate of soda/baking soda and ground ginger in a large bowl. Stir in the molasses/turbinado sugar.

In a separate bowl, beat the golden syrup, melted butter, eggs and pumpkin purée together until smooth. Stir into the dry ingredients and mix until everything is fully incorporated. Stir in the chopped stem/candied ginger.

Spoon the mixture into the prepared pan and bake for about 1¼ hours, or until the loaf is risen and golden and a skewer inserted into the centre comes out clean.

Leave the cake to cool in the pan for about 15 minutes, then turn onto a wire rack to cool completely. Serve with butter.

FOR 1 POT OF TEA

3 heaped teaspoons green
　tea leaves
1.5-cm/¾-in. piece fresh
　ginger, sliced
honey, to taste

Warm the teapot, add the leaves and ginger and pour over boiled water. Brew for 5 minutes. Sweeten as desired.

Mint and summer berry iced tea with strawberry and rosewater cream meringues

This is a lovely summer tisane, and not technically a true tea, although you could add green tea to the pot if you wish. Vary the berries according to what's available, but a mixture looks pretty. Don't be too heavy-handed with the sweetening, as the meringues are deliciously and indulgently sweet! Be sure to use unsprayed roses.

4 egg whites
200 g/1 cup caster/
    superfine sugar
1–2 drops pink food colouring
    or grenadine

FOR THE FILLING
300 ml/1¼ cups double/
    heavy cream
2 teaspoons caster/
    granulated sugar
2 teaspoons rosewater
250 g/1 pint strawberries,
    quartered

TO DECORATE
white and pink rose petals
1 egg white, beaten
2 tablespoons caster/
    granulated sugar

*2 baking sheets, lined
    with baking parchment*
an electric hand whisk
a piping/pastry bag (optional)

MAKES 8–10

Preheat the oven to 150°C (300°F) Gas 2.

Whisk the egg whites in a scrupulously clean bowl until firm (unless you're training for the Olympics, an electric hand whisk is probably best for this). Add the sugar about a tablespoon at a time, and keep whisking until all the sugar has been incorporated. Gently fold in the food colouring.

Using two spoons (or a piping/pastry bag if preferred), place small dollops on the prepared baking sheets, spaced a little way apart. Bake for about 20 minutes, then switch off the oven. Leave the meringues in the oven until cold.

In the meantime, whisk the cream, sugar and rosewater together, until the cream has thickened. Dip the rose petals lightly into the egg white, then gently into the sugar to coat. Leave to dry.

Sandwich the meringues together with the cream and strawberries and pile them onto a serving platter. Scatter over the rose petals and serve.

FOR 1 POT OF TEA

1 large bunch fresh mint,
    plus extra to serve
caster/granulated sugar,
    to taste
ice cubes, to serve
250 g/9 oz. mixed summer
    berries

Put the mint in a teapot and pour over boiling water. Muddle the leaves (as if you were making a mojito) and leave to cool and infuse. Pour into a glass jug/pitcher and refrigerate until very cold. Remove the leaves and pour into 4 tall glasses. Add ice cubes, summer berries and mint leaves and serve with straws.

Lemongrass tea with pistachio and almond baklava

Sticky-sweet baklava make a great treat for anyone with a sweet tooth. Often paired with strong coffee, they taste divine with a gently perfumed cup of lemongrass tea, too. When you have poured the first cup, repeat the brewing process – there should still be enough flavour to produce a second cup. I love this as it is, but those with a sweet tooth could add a little honey. Sometimes I use white or green tea as a base, but the lemongrass alone makes a very special tea.

300 g/2 cups pistachio nuts, roughly chopped
50 g/scant ½ cup ground almonds/almond meal
2 teaspoons ground cinnamon
200 g/6½ oz. filo/phyllo pastry dough
150 g/1 stick plus 2 tablespoons butter, melted
grated zest and juice of 2 large oranges
juice of 1 lemon
200 g/1 cup caster/granulated sugar
seeds from 2 cardamom pods
seeds from 1 vanilla pod

an 18 x 30-cm/7 x 12-in. roasting pan or rectangular cake pan, lightly greased

MAKES 16

Preheat the oven to 180°C (350°F) Gas 4.

Mix the pistachios, almonds and cinnamon together and set aside.

Layer half the filo/phyllo pastry in the pan, brushing each sheet with melted butter as you go. Scatter the nuts evenly over the pastry. Cover with the remaining pastry, brushing each sheet with melted butter as before. Brush the top with melted butter and tuck the edges of the pastry in around the edges. Carefully cut a diamond pattern into the pastry. Bake for 20 minutes, then reduce the oven temperature to 150°C (300°F) Gas 2. Bake for a further 10–15 minutes or so, until crisp and golden.

Meanwhile, place the orange juice and zest, lemon juice, sugar, cardamom, vanilla seeds and pod and 200 ml (¾ cup) water in a saucepan and heat until the sugar has melted. Bubble for 3–4 minutes, until the mixture is slightly syrupy. Leave to cool.

Remove the baklava from the oven. Remove the vanilla pod from the syrup and pour the syrup evenly over the baklava. Leave for several hours and allow the syrup to soak into the pastry. Cut into diamonds and serve.

FOR 1 POT OF TEA

4–5 long stems lemongrass
floral honey, to taste

Give the lemongrass stems a good bash with a rolling pin and cut them into slices about 5 mm (¼ in.) thick. Place them in a teapot and fill with boiling water. Stir well and leave to infuse for 3–4 minutes. Pour into cups and sweeten with floral honey, if desired.

Ti kuan yin tea with Egyptian basbousa

This is a very unusual but no less lovely combination: dense, sticky Egyptian basbousa and a slightly smoky, nutty oolong tea that is one of China's most appreciated. Ti kuan yin comes from the Fujian province and is also called Tie guan yin, which means 'Iron Goddess of Mercy'. The first time I tried it, I was puzzled by its distinctive smell and found it hard to pinpoint just what it reminded me of. Later, when researching suppliers, I read a description saying the tea has notes of toasted walnut and kale/collard greens – and the penny dropped! Please don't let that put you off, though, as it really is a delicious tea and makes a great partner for the sticky-sweet diamonds that are Arabic basbousa. I've made my basbousa slightly less sweet than the traditional version, but unless you have a remarkably sweet tooth, I'm sure you'll still find it sweet and sticky enough!

FOR THE BASBOUSA

225 ml/scant 1 cup full-fat plain yogurt

150 g/1⅓ cups ground almonds/almond meal

185 g/1½ sticks butter, melted

225 g/1 cup plus 2 tablespoons caster/granulated sugar

300 g/2¼ cups semolina

a pinch of salt

1½ teaspoons baking powder

finely grated zest of 1 lemon

FOR THE SYRUP

150 g/¾ cup caster/granulated sugar

juice of 1 lemon

a 20 x 30-cm/8 x 12-in. rectangular roasting dish or cake pan, lightly greased

MAKES 16

Preheat the oven to 180°C (350°F) Gas 4.

Put all the ingredients for the basbousa in a large bowl and beat until smooth. Pour the mixture into the prepared pan and bake for about 30 minutes, until golden and set.

In the meantime, put the sugar, 100 ml (⅓ cup) water and lemon juice in a saucepan and heat until the sugar has melted. Bubble for 4–5 minutes until thick and syrupy. Remove from the heat and leave to cool.

Remove the cake from the oven and pour the cold syrup evenly over the top. Return to the oven for a couple of minutes.

Cut into diamonds and serve.

FOR 1 POT OF TEA

2–3 tablespoons Ti kuan yin leaves

sugar or honey, to taste

Warm the teapot and add the leaves. Add slightly cooled boiled water and leave to brew for 4–5 minutes. Sweeten with sugar or honey as desired.

Gyokuro tea with fudgy dark chocolate and almond cakes

Gyokuro tea is one of Japan's finest teas. The leaves have a higher concentration of chlorophyll, which give them a vivid green colour and a sweet, pronounced flavour. They are steamed to prevent oxidization. It's important to allow the boiled water to cool before brewing, or the delicate flavour will be compromised. Chocolate and almond cake makes a really superb combination with this impressive tea.

250 g/2 sticks soft butter
350 g/1¾ cups caster/
    superfine sugar
6 eggs, beaten
150 g/1 cup plus 2 tablespoons
    plain/all-purpose flour
150 g/1⅓ cups ground almonds/
    almond meal
1 teaspoon almond essence

FOR THE FUDGE TOPPING
180 g/scant 1 cup caster/
    granulated sugar
100 g/6½ tablespoons butter
250 g/8 oz. dark chocolate
150 ml/⅔ cup evaporated milk

*a 20 x 30-cm/8 x 12-in. deep
    roasting pan or cake pan,
    lightly greased*

MAKES 15

Preheat the oven to 180°C (350°F) Gas 4.

Beat the butter and sugar together until light and fluffy. Add the eggs a little at a time until the mixture is smooth (you may have to add a little flour in between each addition to prevent curdling). Stir in the remaining flour, almonds and almond essence. Spoon into the prepared pan and bake for about 50 minutes, until risen and golden. Leave to cool in the pan.

In the meantime, make the fudge topping. Place all the ingredients into a saucepan and heat until the sugar has dissolved and the butter and chocolate have melted. Simmer over gentle heat for 3–4 minutes, until the mixture thickens. Beat for 2–3 minutes until glossy, then refrigerate until cold.

Spread the filling over the cold cake. Cut into squares and serve.

FOR 1 POT OF TEA

4–5 teaspoons Gyokuro
    tea leaves
sugar or honey, to taste

Warm the pot and add the tea leaves. Boil the water and leave it to cool to about 60°C (140°F), then pour it over the tea leaves. Brew for 3–4 minutes. It can be steeped again a couple of times, but the subsequent brewing times should be shorter.

AFTERNOON TEAS

Taking time out in the afternoon to enjoy a pot of tea and a sweet treat should be something we do much more often. It's definitely a good time for sharing something special to eat with the people we care about, without the formality of having to prepare a full meal. Whether it's a full-flavoured gunpowder tea with a slice of sticky walnut tart enjoyed by the fire on a cold winter's day, or an al fresco indulgence of lime iced tea with pretty borage flower ice cubes and irresistible cherry and blueberry eccles cakes in the summer. It's the tea and cake equivalents of chicken soup for the soul.

Lime iced tea with borage ice cubes and cherry and blueberry eccles cakes

White tea complements the refreshing flavour of fresh lime in this lovely summer infusion. Borage-flower ice cubes are wonderful to keep in the freezer: add them to ice teas, cold drinks and cocktails for a special touch. Traditional Eccles cakes were always a favourite in my house – my mum made the best ones!

500 g/1 lb. pitted/stoned cherries
1 teaspoon arrowroot
120 g/⅔ cup caster/
    granulated sugar
150 g/1 cup blueberries
425 g/15 oz. ready-rolled
    puff pastry dough

MAKES 8

Preheat the oven to 200°C (400°F) Gas 6.

Put the cherries in a saucepan with 3 tablespoons water. Cook over gentle heat until the juices ooze. Mix the arrowroot with 4 tablespoons cold water and add this to the cherries, stirring all the time, so that the mixture thickens without becoming lumpy. Add 100 g (½ cup) of the sugar and cook for 2–3 minutes. Stir in the blueberries and leave to cool.

Meanwhile, cut eight 6-cm (2½-in.) rounds from the puff pastry. Put a small spoonful of the fruit in the centre of each round. Moisten the edges with water and gather the pastry up and around the filling. Crimp the edges together firmly to seal them, then gently turn it over so the seam is on the bottom. Repeat with the other pastry circles and arrange on a baking sheet.

Brush the surface of each cake with water, and then dust with the remaining sugar. Bake for about 15 minutes, until golden. Serve slightly warm or cold.

FOR 1 POT OF TEA

4 bags white tea
    (or use fresh leaves)
3 limes, thinly sliced
fresh mint leaves, to serve
honey or caster sugar, to taste

FOR THE ICE CUBES
a handful of borage flowers
an ice cube tray

Several hours beforehand, put the borage flowers in ice cube trays, fill with water and freeze. Warm a teapot. Add the tea and 2 of the limes and fill with boiling water. Brew for 4–5 minutes. Pour into tea glasses, add an extra slice of lime and some mint leaves, and sweeten if desired.

White tea with buttery carrot and orange cake

Life beyond breakfast tea has truly been one of the most amazing discoveries I have made in recent years, but sometimes – when I'm in a hurry or a little preoccupied, and I just need to stick a tea bag in a cup – the box of white tea bags I keep in the cupboard is a godsend. I like the Twinings white tea bags, which make an elegant, quite delicate, very drinkable cuppa, but there are lots of other nice brands out there. Carrot cake is always a favourite; this one is made with butter, and has a lovely flavour and lightness. I've topped it with sweetened mascarpone, which I find is less cloying than the traditional cream cheese frosting. I've also used orange zest to decorate, although sometimes I make little baby carrots out of coloured marzipan or fondant icing.

250 g/2 sticks soft butter
250 g/1¼ cups golden caster/
    granulated sugar, plus
    extra for dusting
4 eggs, beaten
300 g/2⅓ cups self-raising/
    rising flour
2 large carrots, peeled
    and grated
2 teaspoons ground cinnamon
grated zest and juice of
    1 orange
50 g/⅓ cup sultanas/
    golden raisins

FOR THE TOPPING
50 g/3 tablespoons mascarpone
100 g/½ cup caster/
    superfine sugar
zest of 2 oranges, cut into fine
    slivers or shavings

a 20 x 30-cm/8 x 12-in.
cake pan, greased

MAKES 15

Preheat the oven to 180°C (350°F) Gas 4.

Cream the butter and sugar together until light and fluffy. Beat in the eggs a little at a time, until the mixture is smooth. You can add a little flour in between each addition if the mixture seems to be curdling.

Stir in the remaining flour, grated carrot, cinnamon and orange juice and zest. Add the sultanas/golden raisins and stir until everything is fully incorporated. Spoon the mixture into the prepared pan and bake for 35–40 minutes, until risen and golden. Dust with a little more sugar and leave to cool in the pan.

To make the topping, beat the mascarpone and sugar together. Cut the cake into squares and decorate with little dollops of the mascarpone mixture and a little orange zest.

FOR 1 POT OF TEA

3 white tea bags

Warm the pot and add the tea. Pour over water that has been boiled and cooled very slightly. Leave to infuse for 5 minutes before serving.

Pu-erh tea with lemon fudge slices

Pu-erh tea is a fermented dark tea from Yunnan province in China. It goes back hundreds of years, and was once an everyday, affordable tea, but is now relatively expensive. It's a very pleasant tea with a distinctive aroma, and has a reputation for aiding weight loss. Not so much for me, maybe because I like to drink it with these irresistible lemon fudge slices...

FOR THE BASE
200 g/1¾ sticks butter
200 g/1⅔ cups plain/
   all-purpose flour
100 g/¾ cup rice flour
100 g/½ cup caster/
   superfine sugar

FOR THE TOPPING
600 ml/2½ cups double/
   heavy cream
300 g/1½ cups caster/superfine
   sugar, plus extra for dusting
4 eggs, beaten
100 g/¾ cup plain/
   all-purpose flour
grated zest and juice
   of 4 large lemons

*a deep 20 x 25-cm/8 x 10-in.
   roasting pan or cake pan,
   greased and lined with
   baking parchment*

MAKES 15

Preheat the oven to 180°C (350°F) Gas 4.

For the base, rub the butter, flour and rice flour together until the mixture resembles fine breadcrumbs. Add the sugar and bring it together to form a smooth dough. Push the mixture into the prepared pan in an even layer and smooth with the back of a spoon. Bake for about 15 minutes, until firm and golden.

In the meantime, make the topping. Whisk the cream, sugar and eggs together. Slowly add the flour and whisk until smooth. Add the lemon zest and juice.

Remove the cooked base from the oven and immediately pour on the lemon mixture. Return to the oven and bake for a further 20–25 minutes, until the topping is set. Remove from the oven and leave to cool completely. Dust lightly with sugar and cut into bars.

FOR 1 POT OF TEA

3–4 teaspoons pu-erh
   tea leaves
sugar or honey, to taste

Warm the pot and add the tea leaves. Pour over boiled, slightly cooled water and leave to brew for 4–5 minutes. Sweeten to taste with sugar or honey.

Autumn tea with vegan brownies

The best tea companies all have their own special blends, but teas designed for particular times of the year such as summer, autumn/fall and Christmas are very popular. I like the teas of Betjeman & Barton – they have a lovely autumn/fall blend that contains dried pieces of quince, figs, raisins and hazelnuts. These dark, dense brownies are sure to delight chocolate-loving vegans, but I think they will also surprise conventional brownie fans too. They're fab served with a cuppa.

200 g/7 oz. dark/bittersweet
   chocolate, melted
250 ml/1 cup plus 1 tablespoon
   just-boiled water
100 ml/⅓ cup plus 1 tablespoon
   sunflower oil
375 g/2 cups minus 2 tablespoons
   light brown muscovado sugar
1 teaspoon cider vinegar
2 teaspoons vanilla bean paste
175 g/1⅓ cups plain/
   all-purpose flour
½ teaspoon baking powder

a 30 x 17 x 2.5 cm/
11¾ x 6¾ x 1 in. brownie pan,
lightly greased and lined
with baking parchment

MAKES 15

Preheat the oven to 170°C (325°F) Gas 3.

Pour the melted chocolate into a large bowl and slowly whisk in the just-boiled water. Whisk in the sunflower oil. Beat in the muscovado sugar, and then add the cider vinegar and vanilla bean paste. Stir in the flour and baking powder.

Pour the mixture into the prepared pan, and bake for about 45 minutes, until the top of the brownie feels squidgy but set. Leave to cool in the pan, before cutting into squares. Store in an airtight pan, making sure to separate any layers with baking parchment if necessary.

FOR 1 POT OF TEA

4 teaspoons of autumn/fall
   blend tea
sugar and milk, to taste

Warm the teapot and add the tea. Pour on simmering water and let stand for 3–4 minutes. Add milk and sugar as desired.

Tregothnan estate tea with hazelnut, peach and redcurrant frangipane tart

Hidden away on the banks of the River Fal in Cornwall lies the Tregothnan Estate, the family home of Lord Falmouth since 1335. For centuries, Tregothnan's astounding micro-climate has supported many extraordinary species of fruit trees and an enormous range of rare plants. In recent years it has been producing the very first English teas, and they are fast gaining fans – as far away as China and beyond! Hazelnut makes a lovely frangipane-style base for this peach and redcurrant-topped tart, although you could easily vary the fruit according to season.

FOR THE PASTRY
175 g/1½ sticks butter
50 g/¼ cup caster/
   superfine sugar
a pinch of salt
1 egg yolk
250 g/2 cups plain/
   all-purpose flour,
   plus extra for dusting

FOR THE FILLING
200 g/1¾ sticks soft butter
200 g/1⅓ cups toasted hazelnuts,
   finely chopped
200 g/1 cup caster/
   superfine sugar
a pinch of salt
2 eggs
6 ripe peaches
150 g/generous 1 cup redcurrants
100 ml/6 tablespoons apricot
   jam/jelly, sieved

*a 23-cm/9-in. tart pan
   with removable base*

SERVES 8

Preheat the oven to 170°C (325°F) Gas 3.

Beat the butter, sugar and salt together until smooth. Add the egg yolk and stir until thoroughly combined. Fold in the flour and bring the mixture together to form a smooth dough. Wrap in clingfilm/plastic wrap and leave to rest in a cool place while preparing the filling.

Beat the butter, hazelnuts, sugar, salt and eggs together until smooth.

Roll the pastry out on a lightly floured surface and use it to line the tart pan. Spoon the hazelnut filling evenly into the base. Bake for about 30 minutes, until the filling is firm in the centre.

Cut the peaches in half, remove the stone/pit and cut each one into 8 slices. Arrange over the top of tart in slightly overlapping concentric circles, starting at the outside edge. Scatter over the redcurrants. Warm the apricot jam/jelly slightly and stir in 1 tablespoon hot water. Brush it carefully over the top to glaze. Leave to cool and serve in slices.

FOR 1 POT OF TEA

3–4 teaspoons Tregothnan
   Estate tea
sugar or honey, to taste

Warm the pot and add the tea. Pour over boiling water and leave to brew for 3–4 minutes. Sweeten with sugar or honey, as desired.

Lady Grey tea with raspberry macarons

Lady Grey tea is related to the celebrated Earl Grey; it is also a black tea scented with oil of bergamot, but has less bergamot, and also contains lemon and orange oils. It was named in honour of Mary Elizabeth Grey, the wife of the original Earl Grey. Sadly though, romantic notions of Mary Elizabeth sliding effortlessly into the drawing room to sip her namesake tea are misplaced – it was invented in the 1990s! I'm sure that if Lady Mary Elizabeth had been around, she would have given the nod of approval, though, especially if her tea was served alongside these moreish raspberry macarons.

220 g/1¾ cups icing/
confectioners' sugar
160 g/1⅓ cups ground almonds/
almond meal
4 large egg whites
a pinch of salt
95 g/½ cup caster/
superfine sugar
red food colouring gel
200 g/¾ cup high fruit-content
raspberry jam/jelly

a food processor

*2 or 3 baking sheets, lined
with baking parchment*

a piping/pastry bag

MAKES ABOUT 30

Draw 4-cm (1½-in.) circles (spaced a little apart) on the baking parchment as templates so that all the macarons come out the same size; they'll look much prettier when finished.

Blitz the icing/confectioners' sugar and almonds in a food processor until very fine, then push the mixture through a fine-meshed sieve. Set aside.

Whisk the egg whites and salt together until stiff and glossy. Add the sugar, about a third at a time, beating again each time, until the eggs are stiff and glossy and all the sugar has been incorporated.

Carefully but thoroughly fold the almond mixture into the egg whites, until fully incorporated but still light. Fold in enough food colouring to achieve the desired pink colour. Spoon the mixture into a large piping/pastry bag and pipe circles onto the parchment, following the circles you drew earlier.

When all the macarons have been piped, take hold of the baking sheet and tap it firmly on the work surface 2 or 3 times to knock out any air bubbles. Preheat the oven to 140°C (275°F) Gas ½ and leave the baking sheets to stand for 30 minutes.

Bake the macarons for about 15 minutes, until the shells are crisp and they have grown little 'feet'. Remove from the oven and leave to cool. Once completely cool, sandwich with the raspberry jam/jelly and serve.

FOR 1 POT OF TEA

5 teaspoons Lady Grey tea

Warm the teapot and add the tea. Pour in boiling water and leave to brew for 5 minutes or so. Serve with lemon.

Gunpowder tea with walnut tart

FOR THE PASTRY
175 g/1½ sticks soft butter
50 g/¼ cup caster/
    superfine sugar
a pinch of salt
1 egg yolk
250 g/2 cups plain/
    all-purpose flour,
    plus extra for dusting

FOR THE FILLING
50 g/3 tablespoons butter
100 g/½ cup soft brown sugar
100 g/scant ½ cup set honey
a pinch of salt
150 ml/⅔ cup double/
    heavy cream
2 eggs, beaten
225 g/1½ cups walnut pieces

*a 23-cm/9-in. tart pan with
    removable base*

SERVES 6–8

Preheat the oven to 170°C (325°F) Gas 3.

Beat the butter, sugar and salt together until smooth. Add the egg yolk and stir until thoroughly combined. Fold in the flour and bring the mixture together to form a smooth dough. Wrap in clingfilm/plastic wrap and leave to rest in a cool place while preparing the filling.

Put the butter, sugar, honey and salt in a saucepan and heat until the sugar has dissolved and the mixture is smooth. Add the cream, let the mixture bubble for 3–4 minutes, then remove from the heat and leave to cool. Stir in the eggs and then the walnuts.

Roll out the pastry on a lightly floured surface and use it to line the tart pan. You will have some left over, but it is impractical to make any less; just freeze any leftovers and use them for something else. Bake the pastry case blind for about 10 minutes, until it is light golden and firm. Leave to cool slightly, then pour the filling evenly over the base. Bake for about 30 minutes, until the filling is golden and set. Serve in slices.

FOR 1 POT OF TEA

**3–4 teaspoons tea leaves
sugar or honey, to taste**

Warm the pot and add the tea leaves. Pour over boiled, slightly cooled water and leave to brew for 4–5 minutes. Sweeten as desired.

Gunpowder tea is a green tea that dates back to the Tang dynasty of 618–907 AD. It is so named because the leaves are tightly rolled into small balls that were thought to resemble the gunpowder pellets used for cannons, although another theory is that the name comes from the Mandarin term for 'freshly brewed', which is gāng paò dè. Gunpowder tea tends to be quite full flavoured, and is very often used as a base in traditional Moroccan mint tea. Crisp, light pastry wrapping a dark, sticky walnut filling makes this tart one of my favourites (although I admit that I do have a lot of favourites!). I like it served warm, but after a happy accident once, I discovered that when it's refrigerated, the filling turns extra-chewy and delicious, so now that's my little secret treat thing to do with the leftovers.

Russian caravan tea
with crisp vodka cookies

Russian Caravan tea is usually created from a blend of Chinese oolong and keemun. The name comes from the 18th-century camel caravans that travelled the ancient trading routes bringing tea from China, Ceylon and India to Russia. The 6,000-mile journey took over 6 months. In modern blends, a little lapsang souchong is added to give a light smoky finish, as it's thought that the camp fires along the journey may have added a slightly smoky flavour to the tea. I'm not sure if the camel drivers themselves would have drunk much of the tea on this lengthy, unforgiving haul, but I'm fairly sure they would have had the odd nip of vodka along the way. So I created these crisp little vodka-laced cookies in their honour. They're probably not terrifically authentic, but delicious all the same.

125 g/1 cup plain/
   all-purpose flour
50 g/½ cup icing/
   confectioners' sugar
a pinch of salt
90 g/6 tablespoons soft butter
2 teaspoons vodka
icing/confectioners' sugar,
   for dusting

MAKES 12

Preheat the oven to 180°C (350°F) Gas 4.

Put the flour, icing/confectioners' sugar and salt into a large bowl. Rub in the butter until evenly mixed, then add the vodka. Pull the mixture gently but firmly together to form a smooth dough.

Shape the dough into balls the size of walnuts and place on two large non-stick baking sheets, a little distance apart.

Bake for 12–15 minutes until firm and golden. Remove from the oven and transfer to a wire rack to cool. Dust with icing/confectioners' sugar and store in an airtight container.

FOR 1 POT OF TEA

3-4 teaspoons
   Russian Caravan tea
milk, to taste
sugar or honey, to taste

Warm the teapot and add the tea leaves and freshly boiled water. Leave to brew for 5 minutes. Add milk and sweeten with sugar or honey, if desired.

Anhui yellow tea with blackcurrant maids of honour

Yellow tea is one of the rarer types of tea and comes from the Anhui, Sichuan and Hunan provinces in China. Long, slow production gives it a mellow, sweet flavour and makes it the perfect tea to accompany these little blackcurrant-speckled tarts. It's important to choose a good-quality full-fat cheese, full of curds you can get your teeth into – the watery, low-fat versions will spoil the finished tarts. Remove blackcurrants from their stems by running them gently through the tines of a fork.

375 g/12½ oz. ready-rolled
   puff pastry dough
300 g/1¼ cups good-quality
   cottage cheese
50 g/scant ½ cup ground
   almonds/almond meal
50 g/¼ cup caster/
   superfine sugar
finely grated zest of 1 lemon
2 egg yolks
25 g/2 tablespoons butter, melted
100 g/1 scant cup blackcurrants

a 12-cup muffin pan

MAKES 12

Preheat the oven to 200°C (400°F) Gas 6.

Roll the dough out on a lightly floured surface. Cut the pastry into 12 rounds and use them to line the muffin pan.

To make the filling, tip the cottage cheese into a bowl and stir in the almonds, sugar, lemon zest, egg yolks and melted butter. Stir until everything is well mixed. Fold in the blackcurrants. Spoon the mixture into the pastry cases. Bake for about 20 minutes, until the filling is golden and set and the pastry is crisp and brown. Leave to cool slightly before turning out onto a wire rack to cool completely.

FOR 1 POT OF TEA

3–4 teaspoons Anchui
   yellow tea leaves
boiled but slightly
   cooled water

Warm the pot and add the tea leaves. Boil the water and set aside to cool for around 5 minutes. Pour over the cooled water and leave to brew for about 4 minutes. Sweeten to taste with sugar or honey.

Earl Grey tea with Yorkshire curd tart

Earl Grey tea is usually produced from a blend of black China tea with bergamot oil. Bergamot is a citrus fruit that looks like a strange cross between an orange and a lime, and is indigenous to Southeast Asia and southern Italy. I'm a Yorkshire gal, and my dad's favourite dish was Yorkshire curd tart. My mum would buy fresh curds, but nowadays it's not easy to find them. I use cottage cheese, which makes a lovely tart, even if not totally authentic. I bet Earl Grey would have loved a slice...

FOR THE PASTRY
175 g/1½ sticks soft butter
50 g/¼ cup caster/
   superfine sugar
1 egg yolk
250 g/2 cups plain/
   all-purpose flour

FOR THE FILLING
500 g/2 cups cottage cheese
50 g/scant ½ cup ground
   almonds/almond meal
120 g/⅔ cup caster/
   superfine sugar
a pinch of salt
4 eggs, beaten
100 g/6½ tablespoons
   butter, melted
finely grated zest of 2 lemons
100 g/⅔ cup currants
freshly grated nutmeg
icing/confectioners' sugar,
   for dusting

*a 23-cm/9-in. fluted tart pan
   with removable base*

SERVES 8–10

To make the pastry, beat the butter and sugar together until light and fluffy. Add the egg yolk and stir until smooth. Add the flour and work the mixture lightly until it forms a soft dough. Wrap the dough in clingfilm/plastic wrap and leave to rest in a cool place for half an hour, if possible.

Preheat the oven to 180°C (350°F) Gas 4.

Roll out the dough on a lightly floured surface and use it to line the tart pan. There will be some left over, but it will freeze beautifully for another time. Chill the tart case in the freezer while preparing the filling.

Beat the cottage cheese, almonds, sugar, salt and eggs together until smooth. Add the melted butter and lemon zest and beat again. Stir in the currants.

Remove the pastry case from the freezer and bake for about 10 minutes, until biscuit-coloured and firm. Remove from the oven and pour in the filling. Reduce the oven temperature to 150°C (300°F) Gas 2 and bake for about 45 minutes, until the filling has set. Leave to cool in the pan. Dust with icing/confectioners' sugar and serve.

FOR 1 POT OF TEA

3 teaspoons Earl Grey tea
   leaves, or use tea bags
sugar or honey, to taste

Warm the teapot and add the tea leaves. Pour over boiling water. Leave to brew for 5 minutes. Sweeten with sugar or honey, if desired.

Orange pekoe, orange and lemon peel tea with glazed apple cake

I used to buy a blend of orange pekoe with lemon and orange peels from Bettys Café Tea Rooms in Harrogate, North Yorkshire, the much-loved traditional tea rooms that have gained a national reputation for their amazing teas and pastries. The combination has remained a favourite, so I use oven-dried lemon and orange peels, which I remove with a potato peeler and dry in a very low oven whenever I use the juice and not the zest. Aga owners could use the warming oven.

FOR THE CAKE
150 g/1 stick plus
  2 tablespoons soft butter
150 g/¾ cup caster/
  superfine sugar
2 eggs, beaten
150 g/1⅓ cups ground
  almonds/almond meal
50 g/⅓ cup plain/
  all-purpose flour
finely grated zest of
  2 lemons
1 teaspoon baking powder
100 ml/scant ½ cup milk
2 red apples
5 tablespoons apricot jam/jelly

*a 20-cm/8-in. cake pan with
removable base, lightly
greased and lined with
baking parchment*

SERVES 10

Preheat the oven to 160°C (325°F) Gas 3.

Beat the butter and sugar together until light and fluffy. Add the beaten eggs and continue to mix until smooth (you may have to add a little of the flour if the mixture seems to be curdling a little). Add the almonds, flour, lemon zest and baking powder and mix well. Stir in the milk. Spoon the batter into the prepared pan.

Cut the apples in half and remove the core (don't peel them; the skin looks pretty in the finished cake). Cut into thin slices. Starting at the outside edge, arrange the apples in concentric circles, around the cake, slightly overlapping and finishing in the centre.

Bake for about 40 minutes, until the cake is firm and risen and a skewer inserted into the centre comes out clean.

In the meantime, sieve the apricot jam/jelly into a saucepan and add a tablespoon of water.

Remove the cake from the oven and leave to cool for about 15 minutes in the pan. Transfer to a wire rack, brush with the apricot jam/jelly and leave to cool completely.

FOR 1 POT OF TEA

3–4 teaspoons orange
  pekoe leaves
1 teaspoon each dried lemon
  and orange peels
sugar or honey, to taste

Warm the teapot and add the tea leaves and citrus peels. Pour over boiling water and leave to brew for 3–4 minutes. Sweeten with sugar or honey, as desired.

Iced lemon tea with pistachio brownies

Iced tea is normally associated with summer, but it's really nice to keep a jug/pitcher in the fridge all year round because it makes a refreshing cold drink at any time, and with a base of green or white tea, is a healthier alternative to additive-laden fizzy drinks. If you do want a little treat alongside your iced tea, though, these chocolate brownies are dense, delicious and definitely a doddle to make!

250 g/2 sticks butter

500 g/2½ cups caster/
    superfine sugar

100 g/¾ cup cocoa powder

50 g/1½ oz. dark chocolate

4 eggs, beaten

100 g/¾ cup self-raising/
    rising flour

100 g/⅔ cup pistachios,
    roughly chopped

*a 20 x 30-cm/8 x 12-in.
    roasting pan or cake pan,
    lightly greased*

MAKES 15

Preheat the oven to 180°C (350°F) Gas 4.

Put the butter, sugar, cocoa powder and dark chocolate in a large heatproof bowl and set it over a saucepan of gently simmering water over low heat, until the butter and chocolate have melted and the sugar has dissolved. Remove from the heat and leave to cool slightly.

Beat in the eggs, and then fold in the flour. Stir in the pistachios.

Spoon the mixture into the prepared pan and bake for about 40 minutes, until firm but still slightly fudgy.

Leave the brownies to cool in the pan, then cut into squares. Store any leftover brownies in an airtight container.

FOR 1 POT OF TEA

2–3 green or white tea bags

½ lemon, sliced

sugar or honey, to taste

Put the tea bags in a pot with several lemon slices and pour over boiling water. Leave to infuse for 4–5 minutes. Take out the tea bags and add more lemon slices. Leave to cool, then pour into a jug/pitcher and put in the fridge until ready to use. Serve in tall glasses with ice and extra lemon slices.

Esprit de Noël tea with rich fruit cake

Drinking a lovely cup of gently spiced tea is a little like enjoying a glass of mulled wine, so a slice of rich fruit cake to eat alongside makes the perfect partnership. A warm mince pie would be heavenly too! The rich fruit cake is almost the same cake I use as my Christmas cake; it's slightly less spiced, so it's a cake you can enjoy all year round.

FOR THE RICH FRUIT CAKE
300 g/2 cups currants
150 g/1 cups raisins
150 g/1 cup sultanas/
   golden raisins
100 g/⅔ cup natural glacé
   cherries, rinsed and dried
50 ml/3 tablespoons brandy
   or rum
180 g/1⅔ sticks soft butter
180 g/scant 1 cup soft dark
   brown or molasses sugar
3 eggs, beaten
180 g/1½ cups plain/
   all-purpose flour
1 teaspoon ground cinnamon
¼ teaspoon ground nutmeg
finely grated zest of 1 orange

a 23-cm/9-in. cake pan
   with removable base,
   lightly greased and lined
   with a double layer of
   baking parchment

SERVES 10

Put the dried fruit and cherries in a large bowl. Pour over the brandy or rum, and leave the mixture to macerate for a few hours, or preferably overnight.

Preheat the oven to 140°C (275°F) Gas 1. Beat the butter and sugar together until it is light and fluffy. Add the eggs, a little at a time, until they are fully incorporated. You may have to add a little flour in between each addition to stop the mixture from curdling. Stir in the remaining flour, spices and orange zest.

Spoon the mixture into the prepared pan. Line the outside of the pan with a double thickness of newspaper and tie it with kitchen string. This will prevent the cake drying out at the edges during the long cooking time. Bake for about 3½–4 hours. Leave to cool in the pan. If you can leave the cake for a week or so, that's great, but you can also eat it straightaway!

FOR 1 POT OF TEA

3–4 teaspoons Esprit de
   Noel or other Christmas
   blend tea
sugar and milk, to taste

Warm the teapot and add the tea. Pour over simmering water and let the tea steep for 3–4 minutes. Add milk and sugar as desired.

White Darjeeling tea with butter-glazed lemon cake

White Darjeeling tea is produced from the young leaf buds of tea plants grown in the Darjeeling region of the Himalayas. The leaves are fluffy and light, and for this reason you may find it necessary to use more tea than you would normally expect, so for optimum results it's best to follow the manufacturer's instructions when brewing the tea. The lovely, mellow, slightly sweet tea is absolutely spot-on to slurp with this moist, lemony butter-glazed cake. One cup is never enough for me, and one slice invariably turns into two.

200 g/1¾ sticks soft butter
300 g/2½ cups caster/
   superfine sugar
a pinch of salt
3 eggs, beaten
320 g/2½ cups plain/
   all-purpose flour
1 teaspoon baking powder
200 ml/¾ cup plain yogurt
grated zest of 2 lemons
juice of 1 lemon

FOR THE BUTTER GLAZE
30 g/2 tablespoons butter
a pinch of salt
50 g/¼ cup caster/
   superfine sugar
juice of 1 lemon

a 900-g/2-lb. loaf pan, lightly
   greased and lined with
   baking parchment

MAKES AROUND
10 SLICES

Preheat the oven to 180°C (350°F) Gas 4.

Beat the butter, sugar and salt together until light and smooth. Add the beaten eggs a little at a time, until fully incorporated. If the mixture starts to curdle, simply add a little of the flour and stir in.

Add the remaining flour and baking powder, and stir well. Sir in the yogurt, and then the lemon zest and juice.

Spoon the mixture into the prepared pan and bake for about 1 hour 10 minutes, until golden and risen. A skewer inserted into the centre of the cake should come out clean.

Meanwhile, put the butter, salt, sugar and lemon juice into a small saucepan and heat for 3–4 minutes, until the sugar has dissolved and the mixture is syrupy. Pour over the hot cake.

Leave the cake to cool in the pan for 15 minutes or so, then turn onto a wire rack to cool completely.

FOR 1 POT OF TEA

about 6 teaspoons white
   Darjeeling tea leaves

Warm the pot and add the tea. Pour over water that has been boiled but cooled very slightly. Leave to infuse for 5 minutes or so before serving.

DINNER PARTY TEAS

Dinner parties don't always have to end with coffee. Matching teas with desserts and after-dinner treats is becoming increasingly popular, and can mean a light and truly luscious end to an evening. With its gentle, lemony flavour, lemon verbena tea makes a great alternative to coffee – add a slice of lemon ricotta tart and you have a fabulous finale to any meal, and that's just one of the mouth-watering combinations that follow.

Korean yellow tea with Breton prune cake

It's quite a few years since I first tasted traditional Normandy Breton cake filled with sticky prune jam/jelly and fell in love with it, but it remains one of my favourites. If you're not a prune fan, you can substitute other jams/jellies; just make sure they have a high fruit content. Yellow tea has a sweet, mellow flavour that complements the rich cake perfectly.

FOR THE DOUGH
450 g/3⅔ cups plain/
   all-purpose flour
300 g/2½ sticks soft butter
225 g/1 cup plus 2 tablespoons
   caster/superfine sugar
6 egg yolks
1 tablespoon rum

FOR THE FILLING
450 g/16 oz. good-quality
   prune jam/jelly
1 egg yolk, beaten with
   1 tablespoon milk

*a 23-cm/9-oz. springform
   cake pan, lightly greased*

a food processor or stand mixer

SERVES 8–10

Preheat the oven to 190°C (375°F) Gas 5.

Place all the dough ingredients in a food processor or mixer and mix until you have a smooth, soft dough. Shape the dough into a ball, wrap in clingfilm/plastic wrap and chill for 1 hour.

Press half the dough into the prepared pan. Spread the jam/jelly over it in an even layer. Carefully cover the jam/jelly with the remaining dough. Brush the dough with the egg glaze and score a diamond pattern in the surface with a sharp knife.

Bake for 15 minutes, then turn the oven down to 180°C (350°F) Gas 4 and bake for a further 40 minutes, until firm and golden.

Leave to cool in the pan, then serve in slices.

FOR 1 POT OF TEA

3–4 teaspoons yellow tea leaves
boiled, slightly cooled water
sugar or honey, to taste

Warm the pot and add the tea leaves. Boil the water and set aside to cool for around 5 minutes. Pour over the cooled water and leave to brew for about 4 minutes. Sweeten to taste with sugar or honey. Milk would spoil this tea.

Jasmine tea with sticky rice cake

For many of us, jasmine tea represents our first experience of Chinese tea. Sadly, many commercial jasmine teas are made with low-grade tea, artificially flavoured with jasmine oils or chemically compounded jasmine flavours, and are relatively inexpensive. Try to look for good quality green tea or white tea to which freshly picked jasmine flowers have been added. This sticky rice cake makes a lovely change from traditional flour-based cakes, and is great if you ever need to produce a sweet treat that is gluten-free.

150 g/¾ cup sushi rice
300 ml/1¼ cups coconut milk
450 ml/1¾ cups whole milk
a pinch of salt
6 kaffir lime leaves
150 g/¾ cup caster/
    superfine sugar
grated zest and juice
    of 1 lemon
3 egg yolks
2 egg whites

*a 23-cm/9-in. springform
    cake pan, lightly greased*

SERVES 15

Put the sushi rice in a saucepan with the coconut milk and whole milk. Stir in the salt, the lime leaves and sugar.

Cook over very gentle heat for about 25 minutes, until the rice is soft. Remove from the heat and leave to cool. Remove the lime leaves.

Preheat the oven to 150°C (300°F) Gas 1.

Stir the lemon zest and juice. Stir in the egg yolks. Whisk the egg whites to fairly stiff peaks. Fold half the whipped whites into the rice mixture to loosen it, then gently fold in the remaining whites.

Spoon the mixture into the prepared pan and bake for 50 minutes, until set and golden.

FOR 1 POT OF TEA

3–4 teaspoons jasmine tea
sugar or honey, to taste

Warm the pot and add the tea leaves. Pour over boiled, slightly cooled water and leave to brew for 5 minutes. Sweeten with sugar or honey as desired.

Rose Conjou tea with rose geranium and muscat cake

Rose Conjou tea is usually produced from Chinese black tea infused with oil of roses. The black tea leaves are layered several times with rose petals until the natural oils impart the required flavour, creating a really special tea. This glorious dessert cake also takes on the beautiful scent and flavour of roses, imparted by scented geranium leaves (which incidentally are edible). A hefty dousing in gloriously good orange muscat wine makes this cake even more special. End a lovely summer supper with this sublime dessert accompanied by Rose Conjou tea, rather than the more traditional after-dinner coffee.

about 14 small rose-scented
   geranium leaves
250 g/2 sticks soft butter
250 g/1¼ cups caster/superfine
   sugar, plus extra for dusting
a pinch of salt
4 eggs, lightly beaten
150 g/1 cup plus 2 tablespoons
   self-raising/rising flour
100 g/⅔ cup ground almonds/
   almond meal
50 g/⅓ cup fine polenta
   or semolina
250–300 ml/1–1¼ cups
   Brown Brothers Orange Muscat
   and Flora wine

a 23-cm/9-in. springform
   cake pan, greased, lined
   with baking parchment
   and greased again

SERVES 10–12

Preheat the oven to 180°C (350°F) Gas 4.

Carefully arrange the geranium leaves around the outside edge of the prepared pan, close together and with the upper side facing outwards. Set aside.

Beat the butter, sugar and salt together until light and fluffy.

Add the eggs a little at a time until fully incorporated. Add the dry ingredients and beat until smooth. Spoon into the prepared pan, taking care not to dislodge the geranium leaves. Bake for about 40 minutes, until golden and springy to the touch.

Remove from the oven and leave to cool for 5 minutes. Pour the muscat wine all over the cake. Leave to cool completely before turning out onto a cake plate. Scatter the top with sugar and serve in slices.

FOR 1 POT OF TEA

5 teaspoons Rose Conjou
   tea leaves

Warm the teapot and add the tea leaves. Pour in slightly cooled boiled water and leave to brew for 3–5 minutes. Pour into cups and serve.

Silver needle tea with fraises-des-bois friands

Silver needle white tea has an exquisite sweet, delicate and distinctive flavour and is my very favourite of all teas. It is made from the very tips of the tender, downy buds of tea bushes grown on remote mountainsides in the Fujian Province of south east China. The tips are harvested by hand, for only a few days each year. When you see the tea leaves, they do look like fine, velvety little silver needles. Silver needle tea is high in antioxidants and low in caffeine, so it makes a perfect after dinner drink. I've paired it with moist and moreish friands, made special by the addition of tiny woodland strawberries – a marriage made in heaven I think.

70 g/½ cup ground almonds/
    almond meal
30 g/¼ cup plain/all-purpose flour
a pinch of salt
120 g/1 cup icing/confectioners'
    sugar
100 g/6½ tablespoons butter
3 egg whites
80 g/3 oz. fraises des bois

6 friand moulds, lightly greased

MAKES 6

Preheat the oven to 180°C (350°F) Gas 4.

Mix the almonds, flour, salt and sugar in a large bowl.

Melt the butter in a small saucepan, then remove from the heat and leave to cool. Whisk the egg whites until frothy and light (it's not necessary to whip them into peaks as you would if making meringues).

Trickle the butter into the dry ingredients and add half the egg whites. Mix lightly, and then add the remaining egg whites and continue to mix until they are fully incorporated.

Spoon the mixture into the prepared moulds and scatter the fraises des bois over the top. Bake for about 15 minutes or so, until the friands are risen and golden and spring back when pressed lightly.

Serve warm or leave to cool completely.

FOR 1 POT OF TEA

3–4 teaspoons silver needle
    white tea

Warm the teapot and add the tea leaves. Pour in boiled and slightly cooled water and leave to brew for 3–4 minutes. Since silver needle tea has such a lovely naturally sweet flavour, do try it first before reaching for the sugar bowl.

Lemon verbena tea with ricotta tart

Lemon verbena tea has a soft lemon flavour that aids digestion, making it a gentle tea to finish a dinner party. It goes exceptionally well with this lovely, light ricotta tart. You can buy tea bags already infused with lemon verbena, but if you have a plant in the garden you can easily infuse the fresh or dried leaves with boiled water – or use a base of green or white tea to up the antioxidant content.

FOR THE PASTRY
175 g/1½ sticks soft butter
50 g/¼ cup caster/
    superfine sugar
1 egg yolk
250 g/2 cups plain/
    all-purpose flour

FOR THE FILLING
250 ml/1 cup double/
    heavy cream
500 g/2 cups ricotta
200 g/1 cup caster/
    superfine sugar
3 eggs, beaten
grated zest and juice
    of 2 large lemons
icing/confectioners' sugar,
    for dusting

*a 23-cm/9-in. fluted tart pan
    with removable base*

SERVES 8

To make the pastry, beat the butter and sugar together until light and fluffy. Add the egg yolk and stir until smooth. Add the flour and work the mixture lightly until it forms a soft dough. Wrap the dough in clingfilm/plastic wrap and leave to rest in a cool place for half an hour.

Preheat the oven to 180°C (350°F) Gas 4. Roll the dough out to fit the tart pan on a lightly floured surface. There will be some left over, but it will freeze beautifully for another time. Chill the tart case in the freezer while preparing the filling.

To make the filling, beat the cream, ricotta, sugar and eggs together until smooth. Add the lemon zest and juice and beat again.

Remove the pastry case from the freezer and bake for about 10 minutes, until biscuit-coloured and firm. Remove from the oven and pour in the filling. Reduce the oven temperature to 150°C (300°F) Gas 2 and bake for about 45 minutes or so, until the filling has set. Leave to cool in the pan. Dust with icing/confectioners' sugar and serve.

FOR 1 POT OF TEA

3 teaspoons white tea leaves
1 teaspoon dried lemon
    verbena leaves
sugar or honey, to taste

Warm the teapot and add the tea leaves and lemon verbena and pour over boiling water. Leave to brew for 5 minutes. Sweeten with sugar or honey.

Lapsang Souchong tea with whisky fruit tart

Smoky Lapsang Souchong is a little bit of an acquired taste; people either seem to love it or hate it. It's a black tea, from the Fujian province of China, and the smoky flavour and aroma come from the pine fires over which the tea is dried. Good examples of Lapsang Souchong don't have the brash, in your face smell and over-smouldered flavour that cheaper brands do, so if you're going to give this tea a go, do bear that in mind. If you like the thought of a smoky tea now and again, but want a slightly damped-down version, do as I often do, and add just one teaspoonful into a pot of other black tea leaves. A slice of this lovely sticky whisky fruit tart and a cup of smoky tea make a great autumn/fall or winter treat.

FOR THE PASTRY
175 g/1½ sticks soft butter
50 g/¼ cup caster/
    superfine sugar
1 egg yolk
250 g/2 cups plain/all-purpose
    flour, plus extra for dusting

FOR THE TOPPING
200 g/1 cup muscovado sugar
200 g/1¾ sticks butter
80 ml/⅓ cup whisky
4 eggs, beaten
200 g/1⅓ cups currants
200 g/1⅓ cups raisins
100 g/⅓ cup glacé cherries,
    chopped
150 g/generous 1 cup walnuts,
    chopped
caster/granulated sugar,
    for sprinkling
*a 23-cm/9-in. tart pan
    with removable base*

SERVES 8

To make the pastry, cream the butter and sugar together until light and fluffy. Add the egg yolk and beat to combine. Add the flour and bring the mixture together to form a smooth dough. Wrap in clingfilm/plastic wrap and refrigerate for half an hour.

Preheat the oven to 180°C (350°F) Gas 4. Roll the pastry out on a lightly floured surface and line the tart pan with it. You may have some left over, in which case simply freeze it for another time.

To make the topping, put the sugar and butter together in a saucepan and heat until the butter has melted and the sugar has dissolved. Stir in the whisky and leave the mixture to cool a little.

Add the eggs, then stir in the dried fruits and walnuts. Pour the mixture over the pastry base and bake for 30 minutes, or until the topping has set. Sprinkle with caster sugar and leave to cool. Serve in slices.

FOR 1 POT OF TEA

3–4 teaspoons Lapsang
    Souchong tea leaves
sugar or honey, to taste
milk, to taste

Warm the pot and add the tea leaves. Pour over boiling water and leave to brew for 3–5 minutes. Add sugar or honey and milk, as desired.

Ginger and honey tea with gooseberry custard tartlets

FOR THE PASTRY
175 g/1½ sticks soft butter
50 g/¼ cup caster/
  superfine sugar
1 egg yolk
250 g/2 cups plain/
  all-purpose flour

FOR THE FILLING
2 egg yolks
2 whole eggs
300 ml/1¼ cups double/
  heavy cream
50 g/¼ cup caster/
  superfine sugar
3 tablespoons elderflower cordial
200 g/1⅓ cups gooseberries,
  topped and tailed

*eight 5-cm/2-in. tartlet pans
  with removable base*

MAKES 8

Ginger fans will love this tea – there's enough flavour from the ginger to create a zingy, refreshing drink without actually adding tea leaves in any form, but you may prefer the additional depth a little green tea adds. Served with creamy gooseberry and elderflower custard encased in crisp pastry makes a pretty terrific twosome.

For the pastry, cream the butter and sugar together until light and fluffy. Stir in the egg yolk until fully combined. Lightly fold in the flour until the mixture forms a soft, smooth dough. Roll the mixture out to a thickness of about 2 mm (⅛ in.) and cut out 8 rounds about 6 cm (2½ in.) diameter. Line the tartlet pans, taking care to press the mixture into the corners. Refrigerate for 30 minutes.

Preheat the oven to 180°C (350°F) Gas 4. Beat the egg yolks, whole eggs and cream together until smooth. Stir in the sugar and elderflower cordial. Remove the tartlet pans from the fridge and set them on a baking sheet. Scatter a few gooseberries evenly across the base of each one and divide the custard mixture between them, spooning the mixture carefully over the gooseberries. Bake for about 25 minutes, until the filling is set and golden. Leave to cool, turn out of the pans and serve.

FOR 1 POT OF TEA

4 green tea bags, or the
  equivalent in tea leaves
5 cm/2 in. fresh ginger root,
  sliced
a light, flowery honey, such
  as acacia honey, to taste

Warm the teapot and add the green tea and ginger. Fill the teapot with boiling water. Give everything a gentle stir and leave to infuse for 4–5 minutes. Sweeten to taste and pour into cups.

Formosa oolong tea with fig and mascarpone tart

Formosa oolong tea is grown and produced in Taiwan. With its distinctive appearance, taste and aroma, it has earned a place among the world's finest teas. Oolong tea is also alleged to have many far-reaching health benefits. It is believed by many to help aid weight loss too – the caffeine in it supposedly speeds up the metabolism and helps burn extra calories (which is lucky, because that means you can tuck into a slice of this dreamy fig-laden tart without the tiniest trace of guilt).

FOR THE PASTRY
175 g/1½ sticks soft butter
50 g/¼ cup caster/
    superfine sugar
a pinch of salt
1 egg yolk
250 g/2 cups plain/
    all-purpose flour

FOR THE FILLING
50 g/1½ oz. white chocolate,
    melted
250 g/1 cup mascarpone
18–20 fresh, ripe figs
6 tablespoons apricot
    jam/jelly, strained

a 20-cm/8-in. tart pan
    with removable base

SERVES 6–8

Preheat the oven to 180°C (350°F) Gas 4.

Beat the butter, sugar and salt together until smooth. Add the egg yolk and stir until thoroughly combined. Fold in the flour and bring the mixture together to form a smooth dough. Wrap in clingfilm/plastic wrap and leave to rest in a cool place for 30 minutes.

Roll out the pastry and use it to line the tart pan. There will be some pastry left over, but you can freeze the leftovers and use them for something else. Bake the pastry case blind for about 10 minutes or so, until light golden and firm. Leave to cool.

Brush the base of the tart with melted white chocolate and leave it to set. In the meantime, beat the mascarpone gently for a minute or two, until smooth and light. Spoon the mascarpone into the tart and spread it out in an even layer.

Quarter the figs and arrange them vertically in the mascarpone, working in concentric circles and placing them close together, until the pastry case is full and there are no gaps.

Place the jam/jelly in a small saucepan and add 1 tablespoon water. Stir until smooth and gently brush the figs to give them a nice shiny glaze.

FOR 1 POT OF TEA

8 teaspoons Formosa oolong
(Ti Kuan Yin is sublime)

Warm the teapot and add the tea leaves. Boil the kettle and allow the water to cool slightly. Pour the water over the leaves and leave to infuse for 4–10 minutes, to taste.

Index

A

African honeybush tea 47
almonds
  fudgy dark chocolate
    and almond cakes 76
  hazelnut, peach and
    redcurrant frangipane
    tart 88
  lemon and almond
    financiers 56
  pistachio and almond
    baklava 72
Anhui yellow tea 96
apples
  apple and cinnamon
    scones 29
  apple, cinnamon and
    cardamom bourekas
    25
  glazed apple cake 100
apricots: fresh apricot tart
  37
Assam leaf tea 26
autumn tea 87

B

baklava, pistachio and
  almond 72
bananas
  banana and nutmeg
    custard brownies 43
  honey and banana
    bread 51
basbousa, Egyptian 75
basil tea 64
berries: mint and summer
  berry iced tea 71
biscuits
  cardamom shortbread
    55
  raspberry and clotted
    cream whirls 63
black tea 9
  cinnamon-scented
    black tea 67
blackcurrant maids of
  honour 96
blueberries: cherry and

blueberry Eccles cakes
  80
borage ice cubes 80
bourekas, apple,
  cinnamon and
    cardamom 25
breakfast bars, sticky oat
  30
breakfast tea 34
Breton prune cake 110
brewing tea 17–18
brownies
  banana and nutmeg
    custard brownies 43
  pistachio brownies
    102–3
  vegan brownies 87
  white chocolate and
    redcurrant brownies
    64

C

cakes
  Breton prune cake 110
  butter-glazed lemon
    cake 107
  buttery carrot and
    orange cake 83
  caramelized pear and
    thyme cake 52
  Caribbean rum cake 67
  Egyptian basbousa 75
  fat rascals 22
  fraises-des-bois friands
    117
  fudgy dark chocolate
    and almond cakes 76
  glazed apple cake 100
  lemon and almond
    financiers 56
  lemon fudge slices 84
  orange and rosemary
    cake 47
  pistachio brownies
    102–3
  rich fruit cake 104
  rose geranium and
    Muscat cake 114

sticky molasses and
  pumpkin cake 68
sticky rice cake 113
vegan brownies 87
white chocolate and
  redcurrant brownies
  64
caramel
  caramelized pear and
    thyme cake 52
  clotted cream and
    raspberry brulée
    tartlets 44
cardamom pods
  apple, cinnamon and
    cardamom bourekas
    25
  cardamom shortbread
    55
Caribbean rum cake 67
carrots: buttery carrot
  and orange cake 83
chamomile flower tea 40
cherry and blueberry
  Eccles cakes 80
China 17
chocolate
  banana and nutmeg
    custard brownies 43
  fig and mascarpone tart
    125
  fudgy dark chocolate
    and almond cakes 76
  pistachio brownies
    102–3
  vegan brownies 87
  white chocolate and
    redcurrant brownies
    64
Christmas blend tea 104
cinnamon
  apple and cinnamon
    scones 29
  apple, cinnamon and
    cardamom bourekas
    25
  cinnamon-scented
    black tea 67

clotted cream
  clotted cream and
    raspberry brulée
    tartlets 44
  raspberry and clotted
    cream whirls 63
coconut milk: sticky rice
  cake 113
cookies
  crisp vodka cookies 95
  pine nut and rosemary
    cookies 48
  vanilla butter cookies 40
cottage cheese
  blackcurrant maids of
    honour 96
  Yorkshire curd tart 99
crumpets 33
curd tart, Yorkshire 99
currants: Yorkshire curd
  tart 99
custard
  banana and nutmeg
    custard brownies 43
  gooseberry custard
    tartlets 122
  little custard tarts 60

D

Darjeeling tea 107
dried fruit
  fat rascals 22
  rich fruit cake 104
  traditional fruit tea
    bread 34
  whisky fruit tart 121

E

Earl Grey tea 99
  traditional fruit tea
    bread 34
Eccles cakes, cherry and
  blueberry 80
Egyptian basbousa 75
English breakfast tea 34
equipment 12–14
esprit de Noël tea 104

F
fat rascals 22
fennel tea 56
fig and mascarpone tart 125
financiers, lemon and almond 56
Formosa oolong tea 125
fraises-des-bois friands 117
frangipane tart 88
fruit cake 104
fudge slices, lemon 84

G
ginger
    ginger and honey tea 122
    ginger tea 68
    sticky molasses and pumpkin cake 68
goji berry, chia seed and citrus muffins 26
gooseberry custard tartlets 122
green tea 9–10
    ginger and honey tea 122
    ginger tea 68
    iced lemon tea 102–3
    lemon balm tea 44
    mango-infused tippy green tea 37
    manuka honey tea 51
gunpowder tea 92–3
gyokuro tea 76

H
hazelnut, peach and redcurrant frangipane tart 88
honey
    ginger and honey tea 122
    honey and banana bread 51
    manuka honey tea 51
honeybush tea 47

I J
ice cubes, borage 80
iced tea
    iced lemon tea 102–3
    lime iced tea with borage ice cubes 80
    mint and summer berry iced tea 71
India 17
infusers 13
Japan 17
jasmine flowering tea 60
jasmine tea 113

K L
Kaffir lime tea 52
Korean yellow tea 110
Lady Grey tea 90–1
lapsang souchong tea 121
lemon
    butter-glazed lemon cake 107
    Egyptian basbousa 75
    iced lemon tea 102–3
    lemon and almond financiers 56
    lemon fudge slices 84
    ricotta tart 118
lemon balm tea 44
lemon verbena tea 118
lemongrass tea 72
lime iced tea 80
loose leaf tea 17–18

M
macarons, raspberry 90–1
maids of honour, blackberry 96
mango-infused tippy green tea 37
manuka honey tea 51
marmalade
    goji berry, chia seed and citrus muffins 26
    orange and rosemary cake 47

mascarpone
    banana and nutmeg custard brownies 43
    fig and mascarpone tart 125
meringues, strawberry and rosewater cream 71
milk 18
mint
    mint and summer berry iced tea 71
    Moroccan mint tea 25
molasses and pumpkin cake 68
Moroccan mint tea 25
muffins, goji berry, chia seed and citrus 26
Muscat: rose geranium and Muscat cake 114

O
oats: sticky oat breakfast bars 30
olive leaf tea 48
oolong tea 10, 125
orange pekoe tea 22
    orange pekoe, orange and lemon peel tea 100
oranges
    buttery carrot and orange cake 83
    orange and rosemary cake 47
    orange pekoe, orange and lemon peel tea 100
    pistachio and almond baklava 72

P
Pai mu tan tea 55
passion fruit and orange tea 30
pastries
    apple, cinnamon and

cardamom bourekas 25
    blackcurrant maids of honour 96
    cherry and blueberry Eccles cakes 80
    pistachio and almond baklava 72
peaches: hazelnut, peach and redcurrant frangipane tart 88
pears: caramelized pear and thyme cake 52
pine nut and rosemary cookies 48
pistachio nuts
    pistachio and almond baklava 72
    pistachio brownies 102–3
Prince of Wales tea 29
prune cake, Breton 110
pu-erh tea 10, 84
pumpkin: sticky molasses and pumpkin cake 68

R
raspberries
    clotted cream and raspberry brulée tartlets 44
    raspberry and clotted cream whirls 63
    raspberry macarons 90–1
red tea 43
redcurrants
    hazelnut, peach and redcurrant frangipane tart 88
    white chocolate and redcurrant brownies 64
rice: sticky rice cake 113
ricotta tart 118
rooibos red tea: rooibos and vanilla tea 43
rose conjou tea 114

rose geranium and
    Muscat cake 114
rosemary
    orange and rosemary
        cake 47
    pine nut and rosemary
cookies 48
rosewater: strawberry
    and rosewater cream
        meringues 71
royal English breakfast
    tea 34
rum cake, Caribbean 67
Russian caravan tea 95

S
scones, apple and
    cinnamon 29
semolina: Egyptian
    basbousa 75
shortbread, cardamom 55
silver needle tea 117
squeezers, teabag 14
Sri Lanka 17
strainers 14
strawberries
    fraises-des-bois friands
        117

strawberry and
    rosewater cream
        meringues 71

T
Taiwan 17
tarts
    blackcurrant maids of
        honour 96
    clotted cream and
        raspberry brulée
        tartlets 44
    fig and mascarpone tart
        125
    fresh apricot tart 37
    gooseberry custard
        tartlets 122
    hazelnut, peach and
        redcurrant frangipane
        tart 88
    little custard tarts 60
    ricotta tart 118
    walnut tart 92–3
    whisky fruit tart 121
    Yorkshire curd tart 99
tea
    brewing 17–18
    equipment 12–14

history 6–7
    orange pekoe, orange
        and lemon peel tea
        100
    terminology 15
    types of 9–11
tea balls 13
tea breads
    honey and banana
        bread 51
    traditional fruit tea
        bread 34
tea caddies 14
tea cosies 14
tea sticks 13
teabag squeezers 14
teapots 12–13
terminology 15
Ti kuan yin tea 75, 125
traditional fruit tea bread
    34
Tregothnan Estate tea 88

V W
vanilla
    Rooibos and vanilla tea
        43
    vanilla butter cookies 40

vodka cookies 95
walnuts
    walnut tart 92–3
    whisky fruit tart 121
water, making tea 17
whisky fruit tart 121
white chocolate
    fig and mascarpone tart
        125
    white chocolate and
        redcurrant brownies
        64
white tea 10–11, 83
    iced lemon tea 102–3
    kaffir lime tea 52
    lemon balm tea 44
    lemon verbena tea 118
    lime iced tea 80
    silver needle tea 117
    white Darjeeling tea
        107
    white sweet tea (Pai mu
        tan) 55
    white tea pearls 63

Y
yellow tea 11, 96, 110
Yorkshire curd tart 99

Photography credits

**All photography by
Isobel Wield apart from:**

Martin Brigdale 16–17, 78

Catherine Gratwicke 20

Winfried Heinze 38

Debi Treloar 58

Kate Whitaker 108, 128